BVNGALOW · ON THE
ESTATE · OF · WM · H · LINCOLN · ESQ
NEWTON · CENTRE · MASS ·
J · A · SCHWEINFVRTH · ARCHT ·

THE AMERICAN BUNGALOW
1880–1930

Clay Lancaster

DOVER PUBLICATIONS, INC.
New York

To a Noble Brother
JOHN WILLIAM LANCASTER III
Who Shared My Bungalow Childhood

FRONTISPIECE:

Bungalow on the Estate of William H. Lincoln, Newton Centre, Mass. J. A. Schweinfurth, Architect. *American Architect and Building News*, 22 August 1896.

Bibliographical Note

This Dover edition, first published in 1995, is an unabridged republication of the work originally published by Abbeville Press, New York, in 1985.

Library of Congress Cataloging-in-Publication Data

Lancaster, Clay
    The American bungalow, 1880–1930 / Clay Lancaster.
        p.   cm.
    Originally published: New York : Abbeville Press, c1985.
    Includes bibliographical references and index.
    ISBN 0-486-28678-9 (pbk.)
    1. Bungalows—United States—History. I. Title.
NA7571.L36   1995
728'.373'0973—dc20
                                                                            95-34172
                                                                            CIP

Manufactured in the United States of America
Dover Publications, Inc., 31 East 2nd Street, Mineola, N.Y. 11501

CONTENTS

ACKNOWLEDGMENTS

MUCH OF THE RESEARCH on this book was accomplished during 1953 under the auspices of a John Simon Guggenheim Memorial Foundation fellowship. Five years later the subject bore fruit in an illustrated essay, "The American Bungalow," published by the College Art Association in its quarterly, *The Art Bulletin*. The author undertook the balance of the research necessary for this project at the largest single repository of architectural data in the world, Avery Library at Columbia University. The author expresses his gratitude to each of these institutions for its role in making this study possible. In particular he would like to thank Ms. Carol Falcione, of Avery Library, for her patience and efficiency in obtaining needed reproducible illustrations at the recent, final-writing stage.

Credit is due to many of the persons who were helpful in preparing the volume that was the direct result of the fellowship study mentioned above. This is *The Japanese Influence in America*, first published by Walton H. Rawls in 1963, and reissued by Abbeville Press twenty years later. The names of those persons are recorded in both editions of the book. Although the Japanese influence and bungalow movement overlap in the United States, they are distinct phenomena, the latter having its roots in England. Identification of the initial British bungalow—so designated—was made by Dr. Anthony D. King of Leeds. Dr. King included delineations of John Taylor's Birchington bungalow (1872) in his article on this subject that came out in the July, 1973, issue of the *Architectural Association Quarterly*. Five years later he opened a correspondence with the present writer, and my associations with this delightful English scholar have been highly rewarding, including a recent visit and excursion together to bungalow complexes in the area. His sociological viewpoint of the subject suggested the appendix to this opus, which elsewhere has an architectural approach. Dr. King's book, *The Bungalow: The Production of a Global Culture*, was published by Routledge and Kegan Paul in 1984.

Another attractive personality ranking high on the list of recent acquaintances, who has contributed generously to the furthering of this book, is Mr. Randell L. Makinson, Curator of the David B. Gamble House and Greene and Greene Library in Pasadena. Mr. Makinson has kept the author up on recent developments regarding bungalows concentrated in that locale, and he has been most kind and generous in making available new illustrations that were needed.

Others who have given assistance in supplying illustrations in this book include Ms. Mary F. Doherty of the Metropolitan Museum of Art, Ms. Linda J. Cohn of the Art Institute of Chicago, Mr. Adolf K. Placzek, Avery Librarian, Columbia University, and Mr. Jean-Paul Michaux of the New York Public Library. Also for their help in this regard are Ms. Theresa D. Cederholm of the Boston Public Library and Ms. Janann Strand, Greene and Greene docent and author, Pasadena, and Mr. Marvin Rand for use of his excellent photographs.

Finally, the author is again deeply indebted to his good friend and unsurpassable editor, Mr. Walton H. Rawls, for his good advice and numerous suggestions that have gone into the current work, contributing to whatever merits it may have.

Clay Lancaster
Warwick
January 1985

INTRODUCTION

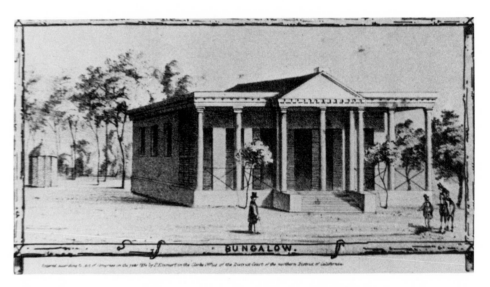

"Bungalow," the Mansion of Theodore Shillaker. Vignette from
P. Emmert, "View of Honolulu from the Catholic Church," Lithograph
Entered in the Clerk's Office of the Northern District of California,
1854. Courtesy of Charles E. Peterson, Philadelphia.

THE AMERICAN BUNGALOW has become a cherished antique, with two to four generations having intervened between its flowering and the present. The bungalow enjoyed the same significance during the first twenty or thirty years of the twentieth century as the cottage had before it, which means that, as a style, it constituted virtually all of the smaller detached houses built during its period. After the singleness of form of Federal architecture during the early nineteenth century, the American cottage had branched into several distinct types under the aegis of the Revival modes. It was made to resemble an ancient Aegean shrine, a medieval English dwelling, an Alpine chalet, or a Mediterranean abode, in declining numbers in the order given. During the Eclectic period of the later nineteenth century, the cottage lapsed into several colonial-manner and "Queen Anne" phases. The bungalow that followed acquired even more diversity, specific examples showing a link with the Japanese temple, Indian rest house, Swiss herdsman's hut, Spanish hacienda, pioneer log cabin, Pompeiian peristyle domus, and even Mississippi steamboat. But these are extremes, as the average bungalow reflected the society that produced and used it and (like that society) displayed no predominant ancestry. Herein lay its first commonality. The second has to do with time. Whereas the American cottage may be said, arbitrarily, to have come into being with the establishment of home rule in the United States and persisted up to the hegemony of the bungalow—a period of approximately 125 years—the full force of the bungalow flourished for only about one-fifth of this span. However, due to the population increase, an urgent need for housing, and rapid expansion across the continent, more bungalows may have been built during this short time than cottages previously. Here resides the true importance of the bungalow: its quick rise to prominence, its nationwide expansion, and its overwhelming numbers, to which may be added its many types and facets, its originality, and its contributions to later American architecture. These traits and its antiquity justify exploring the American bungalow as an art form and as a document reflecting the life of its era.

What has happened to the bungalow? Where is it now? How could a building type that once abounded over such a wide territory have receded so far into the background? These questions in themselves are frank admission that, for the most part, the bungalow has disappeared. It has been the victim of catastrophes such as fire, wrecking crews, and renovators. A great many have been swept away (as has the bulk of our lost architectural heritage) by urban change and expansion. The present encouragement and accommodation of swarms of private vehicles has brought about the widening of streets in older communities, and this has shoved small-lot-sited bungalows into oblivion. They have been replaced by featureless detached houses on land without landscaping, and by mammoth high-rise apartment buildings centered on a block. The destruction of family-size perimeter homes in delightful individual gardens has meant the loss of a portion of true humanity. It has set people seeking false compensations, such as restless travel, incessant amusement, pointless accumulation of gadgets, accessories, and vanities, and, of course, the questionable comforts of the wide range of presently available vices. The artificial environment is conducive to an unnatural life. We tend to overlook this self-evident law today. During the bungalow regime the periodical literature laid stress upon it, and with considerably less cause than we have, since staid Victorians and smug Edwardians—against whom the propaganda was leveled—resorted to considerably fewer excesses than people do today. The bungalow compound was a haven for a man and his family, a place that met all their basic needs. However, despite their manifold enemies in the modern world, bungalows are still around, a good percentage continuing to function in the way they were meant to. We have not been oriented in their direction for such a long time that we have ceased to notice them. But as in the case of other phenomena, with increased interest in bungalows, they will emerge from their extended retreat into obscurity. Some already have come to the attention of the preservation movement. Today, few are referred to as bungalows, the term used by their designers and builders, but increasing familiarity with the nobler aspects of the style and its more remarkable monuments undoubtedly will lead to a reinstatement of the word.

The eventual manifestation of the bungalow (by whatever name it might have come to be called) was inherent in the establishment of a democracy on this continent, the matter being left open as to exactly when and in what manner the appropriate freeman's dwelling was to materialize. Based upon equality, democracy is an effective social leveling device, settling the bulk of the population into the middle financial bracket. The bungalow was conceived specifically for this group, being a house of limited size, adequate for a small family, usually fitted onto a lot of modest proportions, affording an overall effect of hominess, and with its price held down to a figure the average citizen could afford. Although its name was imported, and it continued a movement earlier in force abroad (see Chapter One), the form of the American bungalow was devised for the national temperament, for the New World setting, and for proletarian needs; and it made use of already-established elements here (see Chapter Two).

However, it is not to be assumed that the American bungalow adhered to a limited norm. It was far too versatile for this, as it gathered inspiration from many different sources, adapted itself to widely divergent environmental and climatic conditions, made use of numerous kinds of building materials, and ranged in magnitude from tiny weekend camp shacks to large and luxurious retirement homes. That the application of the word "bungalow" to such architectural diversity suggests great elasticity cannot be denied, but among its number are to be found certain factors providing a common denominator. One must not look for some obvious feature, such as the classic orders in Greek Revival, or late medieval English motifs in Gothic Revival buildings. The bungalow belongs to the modern period, and its borrowings are of principles more than of elements, and of essences rather than of styles. These amalgamate readily as needed and do not interfere with the functional aspects of the building. The foremost physical requirement of any building is shelter, and in the bungalow this is plainly in evidence. It is symbolized in the design importance given to the roof, which usually is low-pitched and extends to deep eaves. Posts, walls, doors, and windows take their places quietly in the scheme, receding into the shadows under the dominant roof. The bungalow is set low to the ground; it nestles into and becomes part of its environment. A special type of planting was devised for the bungalow, and the effect is more picturesque than architectural. Its materials mostly retain their natural color and texture; and unpainted woods, stone, tile, and even stucco and plaster relate to the trees, rocks, and earth of its setting. The bungalow attracts no special attention to itself. It is casual, and it promotes the informal life among those who dwell therein. Not since primitive times, when men fashioned shelters with much the same instinct as beavers build lodges or birds make nests, has the residence been such an intimate part of the natural environment as under bungalow impetus. With such lack of ostentation, is it any wonder that soon after its heyday the bungalow should have become overlooked and forgotten?

The bungalow was succeeded by a number of fads and fashions, only one of which has shown any endurance value, and this one was an outgrowth of the bungalow. Returning servicemen from World War I waxed sentimental over quaint building types seen overseas, and the American suburbs soon were littered with houses having steep gables and nailed-on boards aping half-timber work, labeled "Old English" and "Norman." The reaction was a rediscovery of our own colonial; and Georgian-type brick veneers worked their way westward from the Atlantic seaboard to meet and bypass stuccoed "Montereys" and "Missions" pushing eastward from the Pacific coast. A wave of cold rationalism from Europe next unloaded a mass of stark geometric building blocks on our shores, its only redeeming grace was in prompting Frank Lloyd Wright to design his masterwork, Fallingwater, in this manner. Fallingwater, in western Pennsylvania, avoids the shortcomings of other international-style structures through the incorporation of natural materials, hovering forms, and in harmonizing with its setting—all of which are bungalow characteristics. The unrest and lack of social stability following World War II was symbolized in the split-level house, whose main virtue was in being more human in scale than its contemporary alternative, the high-rise. Yet what was gained by not becoming a monstrous blight on the landscape, even at a distance, was lost through a monotonous sprawling out over vast areas, thus rendering more topography unsightly at close range. Of all types devised after the bungalow period, the one that has persevered is the ranch house. By this name the small American house of the 1960s became best known in England and Europe. It purports to be an adaptation of early Spanish homes of the Southwest and California, but it derives directly from the bungalow (see Chapter Five). We cannot fully understand the small detached house of today until we have established an intimate acquaintance with its forerunners. Considering each in the light of its time, by comparing bungalows with their successors, we shall arrive at a keener insight into the adequacies and shortcomings of both.

Today we have a tremendous fund of information on American architecture from the first white settlements early in the seventeenth century down through late-nineteenth-century Eclecticism. A great deal is in book form as monographs dealing with regional works or a single period over a greater area. There are also digests of these studies. Ample publication (much of it in magazines) has been issued on current building as well. Through library card catalogs and indexes to periodical literature one can be well supplied with data on these two extremes of America's construction program. The gap is in between, especially the first quarter of the twentieth century, the bungalow period. A quantity of illustrated information was issued on the bungalow in its own time and may be exhumed (in those few libraries that keep back copies of periodicals), but most of this record is superficial, for light reading, or had a commercial intent, such as plan books and catalogs for selling designs. Current authors dealing with the era have been limited to two areas: the first is the Chicago School, featuring Frank Lloyd Wright; and the second is the California School, concentrating on the Greene brothers—Charles Sumner and Henry Mather. Wright preferred to call his domestic models "prairie houses," but they are bungalows nonetheless. On the West Coast the term is inescapable, much of the contemporary literature referring to them as "California bungalows," even in publications issued east of the Mississippi River. Due to its prevalence, its period significance, its innovativeness, and its shameful neglect, the time is ripe to investigate the bungalow in depth and assess the movement from an impersonal viewpoint and advantageous perspective.

"Bungal-ode"
by Burges Johnson

There's a jingle in the jungle,
  'Neath the juniper and pine,
They are mangling the tangle
  Of the underbrush and vine,
And my blood is all a-tingle
  At the sound of blow on blow,
As I count each single shingle
  On my bosky bungalow.

There's a jingle in the jungle,
  I am counting every nail,
And my mind is bungaloaded,
  Bungaloping down a trail;

And I dream of every ingle
    Where I angle at my ease,
Naught to set my nerves a-jingle,
    I may bungle all I please.

For I oft get bungalonely
    In the mingled human drove,
And I long for bungaloafing
    In some bungalotus grove,
In a cooling bung' location
    Where no troubling trails intrude,
'Neath some bungalowly rooftree
    In east bungalongitude.

Oh, I think with bungaloathing
    Of the strangling social swim,
Where they wrangel after bangles
    Or for some new-fangled whim:
And I know by bungalogic
    That is all my bungalown
That a little bungalotion
    Mendeth every mortal moan!

Oh, a man that's bungalonging
    For the dingle and the loam
Is a very bungalobster
    If he dangles on at home.
Catch the bungalocomotive;
    If you cannot face the fee,
Why, a bungaloan'll do it—
    You can borrow it of me!

Good Housekeeping Magazine
February 1909, p. 176.

ORIGIN AND MEANING OF THE TERM "BUNGALOW" AND THE INDIAN IMPRINT UPON ENGLISH ARCHITECTURE

THE WORD "BUNGALOW" originated in India, deriving from the Bengali noun *bānglā*, meaning a low house with galleries or porches all around, and identical with the Hindi or Hindustani adjective *banglā*, "belonging to Bengal." Its association with a building type was first made by the English, by those engaged in military, administrative, or trading activities in that great subcontinental adjunct to the British empire. A good deal of their time was spent traveling and living in portable tents or shelters, which often were covered with thatch for insulation from the sun's heat, the thatch itself being called *bangla*. A diary preserved in the India Office, under the date 25 November 1676, notes: "It was thought fitt . . . to sett up Bungales or Hovells . . . for all such English in the Company's Service as belong to their Sloopes & Vessells."[1] Later, in 1711, a reference reads: "All along the Hughley Shore . . . almost as far as the Dutch Bungelow."[2] The spelling here comes closer to ours, but it becomes identical only about a century later. Around 1825 Mary Martha Sherwood, in *The Lady of the Manor*, records: "The bungalows in India . . . are, for the most part . . . built of unbaked bricks and covered with thatch, having in the center a hall . . . the whole being encompassed by an open *verandah*."[3] These were temporary shelters, or caravanserais, sometimes referred to as *dak-*, *dawk-*, or *dāk-bungalows*, the prefix a Hindi or Mahratti word signifying "post" or "relay," thus resthouses. People in the United States became aware of this meaning during the bungalow period: an article in the *American Architect and Building News*, in 1908, characterized the "dāk-bungalow" as "a house for travelers, such as are constructed by the Indian Government at intervals of twelve to fifteen miles on the highroads in many parts of India."[4]

To the British in southern Asia the bungalow was no dream house. J. Lockwood Kipling—father of the poet and raconteur of jungle tales—denounced the bungalow as "about as handsome as a stack of hay" offering "the 'irreducible minimum' of accommodation." It was "a purely utilitarian contrivance developed under hard and limiting conditions."[5] Kipling offered illustrations to buttress his remarks. The bungalow to which he referred consisted of a shallow rectangular platform supporting

1. Early Form of Englishman's Bungalow, from an Illustration in Atkinson's "Curry and Rice." *Country Life in America*, February 1911.

Fig. 1

Fig. 2

Fig. 3

a row of posts, behind which receded the perimeter verandas, and over which rose the pyramidal thatch roof, pierced by a chimney, and from the apex bunching was suspended a ladder that was used for making repairs or dousing fires. Kipling observed that, after the Mutiny of 1857, thatch was prohibited in British cantonments. Roofs then were covered with tile and became lower-pitched. The wall frequently acquired a clerestory, for extra light and ventilation. In that tropic clime, a maximum of air circulation was essential to comfort, and in the later development of complex form, each room was provided with three or four exposures. French doors opened onto the shaded verandas. Interiors were plain. The ceiling was of stretched calcimined calico, which was removable for cleaning. The only hint of elaboration was finials at the extremities of the roof ridge. Another of Kipling's plans, designated a "common form," with thicker walls (indicative of sun-baked bricks) and thatching, is long and shallow, the rooms of equal size and in a row, with anterooms inserted where needed along the area of the rear gallery. The rooms connect one to another or are accessible by means of the encircling piazza. In neither of these examples was attention paid to interest or variety in architectural shapes, subtlety of proportions, space flow, or ease of circulation. Needless to say, it took a long time for the bungalow to make any impression upon the British as a model for dwellings in England.

The veranda was an integral part of the bungalow, but it was associated with less base types of buildings as well. The word occurs in several Indian languages, as Hindi *varandā* and Bengali *vārāndā*, and it has a connection with the Portuguese and older Spanish *varanda* (*baranda*), a railing, "balustrade," or balcony. A British trade paper of 1711 describes an Indian building as being "very ancient, two Story high, and has . . . two large Verandas or Piazzas." Another, of 1757, speaks of: "A penthouse or shed, that forms what is called in the Portuguese Linga-franca *Verandas*, either round, or on particular sides of the house." In other eighteenth-century accounts the spelling varies, appearing as *verander*, *voranda*, *virander*, *feranda*, and even *feerandah*.[6] By 1800 or shortly thereafter (as indicated in Mrs. Sherwood's account—note 3 above) the English had settled on *verandah*, with final "h," which is more in line with the Eastern pronunciation. Unlike the word "bungalow" at that

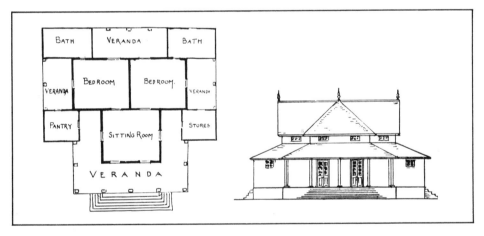

2. Floor Plan and Front Elevation of a Common Form of the Government *Dāk* or Posting Bungalow. *Country Life in America*, February 1911.

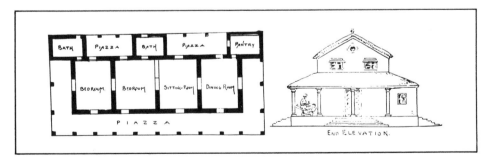

3. Floor Plan and End Elevation of a Common Form of Bungalow that Could be Extended at Will to Include More Rooms. *Country Life in America*, February 1911.

THE AMERICAN BUNGALOW

time, "verandah" had an exotic, status ring to it, and the acquisition of the architectural feature added tone to any habitation.

The first Indian influence in English architecture was a phase of the more general Oriental adopted by the upper classes. It began with the modeling of garden pavilions in the Chinese or Turkish manner, which appeared as appropriate ornaments in English parks, the natural-landscape species of gardening inspired by Sino-Persian prototypes. By way of distinguishing it from the traditional European garden laid out along geometric lines, the French called it the *jardin Anglo-Chinois*.[7] Such conceits were publicized through G. L. LeRouge's *Détails des Nouveaux Jardins à la Mode*, consisting of nineteen portfolios printed at Paris from 1776 to 1787. William Wrighte's *Grotesque Architecture or Rural Amusements*, London, 1790, included six designs (plates 21–24, 26, and 28) of Turkish mosques or Moresque pavilions. The Turkish/Moresque vogue introduced bulbous domes and minarets, thus paving the way for these elements prominent in the Indian Moslem style. The use of Oriental forms during the eighteenth century had been architecturally inconsequential, but the Indian style determined two sizable buildings in England early in the nineteenth century.

The first example was Sezincote in Gloucestershire, the country seat of Sir Charles Cockerell, the design of which was conceived by the builder's brother, Samuel Pepys Cockerell. The brothers had served in India, Samuel as Architect and Surveyor to the East India House. However, the motifs of Sezincote are said to have been derived largely from Thomas Daniell's drawings of Indian architecture. Beginning in 1795, Thomas (and later William) Daniell published, in color, a series of portfolios of views of India, each portfolio containing a set of twenty-four plates, entitled *Oriental Scenery*.[8] Thomas Daniell personally offered suggestions for Sezincote and particularly for the landscaping, in which there was a Hindu bridge.[9] The house or villa itself was of Mughal style. Its main pavilion was rectangular, of golden stone, and crowned by a bulbous dome of green copper. Although the front windows were Georgian, the entrance was set in a high, arched motif, and turrets at the corners were capped by little open pavilions or minarets. The chimneys, too, resembled minarets in profile. A polygonal projecting salon was centered on the garden facade, and here fenestration was *Fig. 4* ample and with lobated heads. An arcade, projecting from the west side, curved as a long orangerie, with an octagon forming the terminus. Enhanced by the beauty of its setting, Sezincote is a successful compo-

4. The South Facade of Sezincote from the Pavilion at the End of the Orangerie. S. P. Cockerell, Architect. *Country Life*, 13 May 1939.

sition; and although Oriental of detail, it is Classic of framework, in accordance with the British genius in architecture.

Architect Humphrey Repton made some contribution to the Cockerell villa, but exactly what it was is uncertain. Coeval with its completion, or in 1805, Repton was called to Brighton to confer with the Prince Regent on renovating and enlarging the classical-style Marine Pavilion (by Henry Holland, 1784) into a lavish exotic palace. Chinese wallpapers presented to the monarch several years earlier had prompted him to order a special gallery built; and subsequently the great domed Saracenic riding arena and stables had been begun by William Porden. Peter Frederick Robinson, architect of William Bullock's Egyptian Hall, a museum in Piccadilly, London, also had worked at Brighton. With the nucleus of an Oriental fantasy started, Humphrey Repton brought it to fruition on paper. When Repton's drawings were shown to him, the Prince was delighted and remarked: ''. . . I consider the whole as perfect, and will have every part of it carried into immediate execution.''[10] But it was not to be: a wave of national economizing caused the project to be laid aside. Repton's bizarre scheme was realized only in that it was published in color, with hinged cutaway views of the original structure overlaying renderings of the elaborate proposals.[11]

The Palace at Brighton, as we know it, was begun in 1815 and completed in 1821. Additional land had been acquired for it, and John Nash, the Surveyor General, became the architect. The outline of the old Marine Pavilion is barely discernible under a conglomeration of domes, minarets, conical roofs, fancy parapets, and trellis gingerbread. The

Fig. 5

end pavilions are entirely of the Nash regime, housing the Banqueting Hall and Music Room. These two interiors have ornamental, high-vaulted ceilings with crystal chandeliers hanging from the necks of flying phoenixes, lamps from the mouths of dragons, painted panels of Oriental scenes in red ''lacquer'' and gold, figures in recesses, pagodas between the windows, wallpaper with yellow dolphins, and a profusion of draperies with birds and mythical beings and hung with fringe and tassels and little bells. Views of the palace were published in 1838, during the reign of Queen Victoria, and included the garden facade here reproduced.[12] The architecture was a symbol of royal pride in the empire's foremost possession.

Sezincote and Brighton were the top specific manifestations of Indian architecture in England, but contemporary with one and preceding the

5. River Facade of the Palace at Brighton. John Nash, Architect.
E. W. Brayley, *Illustrations of Her Majesty's Palace at Brighton*, London, 1838.

other was an imaginary design belonging in the same category. It appeared in Robert Lugar's *Architectural Sketches for Cottages, Rural Dwellings and Villas, in the Grecian, Gothic and Fancy Styles*, London, 1805. Plates XXI–XXXII present plans and a view of a villa in one of the "Fancy Styles," which is Mughal, and about which the author writes: "It is but justice to acknowledge I have taken the idea of the design from one of Mr. Daniell's views of India. It is, I think, by no means unsuitable for an English villa." He fails to mention the lugubrious aspect of his model, which is the "Mausoleum of Sultan Purveiz, near Allahabad."[13] Other "fancy" types were in the Egyptian or Turkish (Plate XXXVI) and Chinese (Plate XXXVIII) taste.

A later book offering an even wider array of Oriental-style buildings was Richard Brown's *Domestic Architecture*, London, [1841]. The range includes a Persian Pavilion, with a tall, columned portico and ample facilities for entertaining (Plate XL), a Chinese Residence with symmetrical wings (Plate XLIII), a Burmese Palital Hall of Assembly (Plate XLV), a Morisco-Spanish Palital Building (Plate XLVII), and an Oriental Pavilion (Plate XLVI), which is Mughal. Like the Persian Pavilion this one shelters a great banqueting room and music saloon, with audience room, divan, library, boudoir, and a central circular rotunda. Although likewise set on a platform, the villa is not compact, as in the case of Lugar's design, but extends left and right, reminiscent of Daniell's "Jummah Musjed, Delhi."[14] Apparently the Lugar and Brown designs were never constructed.

The Sezincote villa, Brighton palace, and the fantasies in the Lugar and Brown books testify to the fact of Indian influence upon English architecture; but they are of such baronial scale and are adorned in such a sophisticated manner that they belong to a different world from that of the bungalow, which is our proper subject.[15] While keeping the national affinities in mind, as bearing upon the subject, let us consider the simple cottage as forerunner to the type designated bungalow in Britain. At the time the Cockerell villa was receiving finishing touches and Repton was showing plans to the Prince Regent, a young renderer in the office of Sir John Soane published two books of plans for plain country buildings. These were *Designs for Cottages, Cottage Farms and Other Rural Buildings*, London, 1805, and *The Rural Architect*, London, 1806. The author–architect was Joseph Gandy (b. 1771), who had been trained at the Royal Academy, a background that was much in evidence in some of the grandiose subjects of his architectural renderings.[16] By contrast, the designs in his books are of the utmost simplicity. Forms are of almost geometric severity, arranged informally, covered by low-pitched roofs with deep eaves casting broad shadows that figure prominently in the architectural pattern, further accented by recesses, the openings unadorned, and supports stripped to structural necessity. Of the three here reproduced, one—from the first book—is for a small tenant house with sections for keeping pigs, poultry, and pigeons, and the other two—from the second—are for a dairy and four attached laborers' cottages. One might think that the humble uses of these buildings would account for their starkness; but, considering the period, normally this would not have been the case. At that time dependents' shelters would have been rustic and stylistically retarded as compared to residences and other structures for the upper classes.

Figs. 6, 7, 8

The Gandy designs were a century ahead of their time. They show the careful composing of the best of bungalows, and one asks: whence came their source of inspiration? Although Gandy experienced some

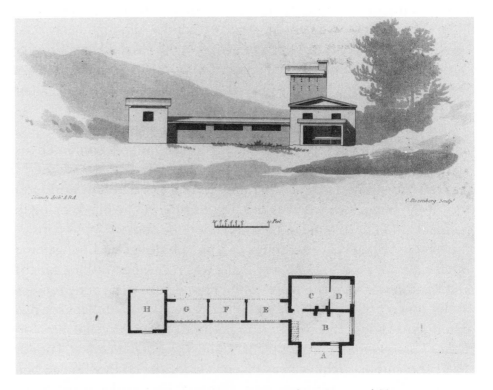

6. Cottage with Conveniences for Keeping Poultry, Pigs and Pigeons. Joseph Gandy, *Designs for Cottages*, London, 1805.

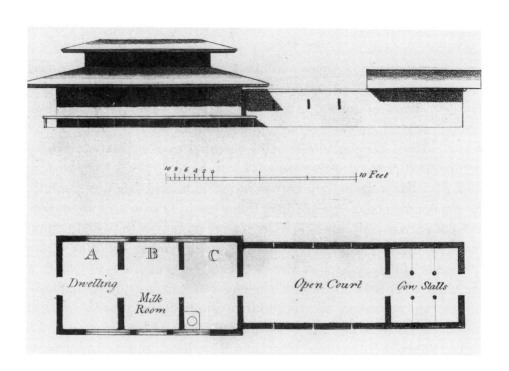

7. Elevation and Plan for a Dairy. Joseph Gandy, *The Rural Architect*, London, 1806.

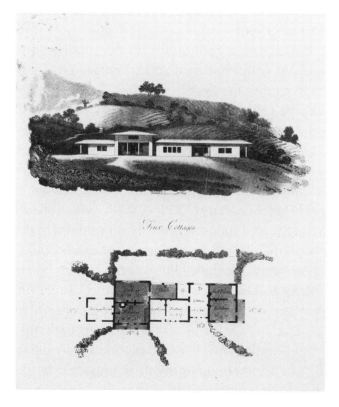

8. Four Attached Cottages. Gandy, *The Rural Architect*.

religious conversion from India, confessing that his object of worship was "the sacred Aum or Om,"[17] it is doubtful that the characteristics of his architecture came from any farther away than the continent of Europe. The most likely source was the idealized primitive hut of the neoclassic theorists. Chief of the group was Marc Antoine Langier, once a Jesuit scholar, who had left the order and become art adviser to princes and municipalities. Langier wrote two influential books, *Essai sur l'Architecture* (1753) and *Observations sur l'Architecture* (1755), lashing sharp criticism against mid-eighteenth-century building design yet offering the means of rectifying it through adhering to reason and logic. Such rationalism was embodied in Gandy's creations for the rural setting. The other fount Gandy drew from was Mediterranean, acquired during 1794 while in Italy, where he had been sent by his father's employer to complete his visual education.[18] The type referred to is the almost insignificant, stucco-walled, tile-roofed habitations dotting the Italian landscape. They had appeared in the paintings of native artists, such as Giotto, Raphael, Titian, Veronese, and Giorgione, and in the canvases of the Frenchmen Poussin and Claude Lorraine.[19] In contrast to the style changes affecting the great buildings from one age to the next, lesser or provincial Italian shelters were built in practically the identical manner since ancient Etruscan times.

The style known as Italianate (a geographic rather than period designation) did much to direct British taste into an acceptance of architectural simplicity, especially during the Regency period. The first example in England was a small villa called Cronkhill, designed by John Nash and built in 1802 for Lord Berwick's agent at Attingham, near Shrewsbury.[20] One can hardly conceive of a greater contrast than this plain building and the elaborate fussiness of Nash's later design for the Brighton palace. Similar in size and character to Cronkhill was a scheme in Robert Lugar's *Architectural Sketches (Plates XXVII–XXVIII)*, which stands in as sharp opposition to the Mughal-mausoleum-villa-on-podium in the same volume as the two Nash manifestations. Another of Lugar's books, *The Country Gentleman's Architect*, London, 1807, offers a plainer house of about equal volume (Plates 6, 14), this one for accommodating farm workers. Plate 4 is of a cottage with appended blacksmith's shop that looks quite indigenous to England; it forms a link between early folk building and the new nineteenth-century work planned by trained architects. The impression of spontaneous growth is imparted by diversities between one part of the building and another: by variations in

Fig. 9

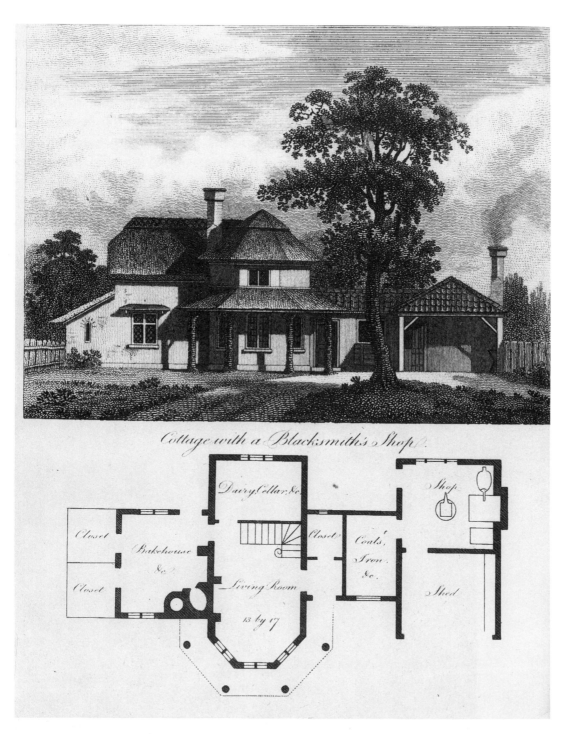

Cottage with a Blacksmith's Shop.

9. Plan and Elevation of a Cottage to Which is Attached a Blacksmith's Shop.
Robert Lugar, *The Country Gentlemen's Architect*, London, 1807.

form, the combining of rectangular and octagonal pavilions, the left part two-storied, the right low; one roof hipped, one gabled, another jerkin-headed, and the inclusion of a lean-to; by the use of different materials, half of the roof being covered with thatch and the balance with tile; and by the use of primitive posts to the porch, rustic tree trunks, nowhere repeated. If this house were to be built in England a century later, because of its traits of small size, partially thatched roof, and veranda encircling the base of one pavilion, it would have been designated a bungalow.

Peter Frederick Robinson, mentioned earlier as having contributed to the Brighton renovation and having served as architect of Egyptian Hall, compiled a house-pattern book called *Rural Architecture*, London, 1823. Many of the designs are of small, heavy-looking cottages, with thick walls, gigantic chimneys, steep thatched roofs, Gothic bargeboards, and quaint porches, that hark back to peasants' cottages of the Middle Ages. A refreshing exception is Design VIII, inspired by a European type

10. Design for a Swiss Cottage. P. F. Robinson,
Rural Architecture, London, 1823.

but quite unlike the Mediterranean coastal house, this one coming from high in the Alps—the Swiss chalet. It is predominantly a wood structure (trees being plentiful in the mountains), and the low-pitched roof is a prominent feature, from which the open galleries or balconies seem to be suspended, and these, with external stairways and great flange brackets, conceal the plain rectangularity of the building proper. Both floors contain two square rooms with fireplaces back-to-back between them, without inner access from one level to the other.[21] Design XIV in the same volume also is labeled Swiss, but it presents an entirely different impression because of the high-pitched roof.[22] The Alpine chalet inspired an example in another of Robinson's publications, *Designs for Ornamental Villas*, London, 1827, which, as the title implies, has to do with much larger residences. Design One depicts a house with some forty rooms and porches on three levels, seeming more like an inn than a private residence. Its entrance lodge—Design Two—contains more domestic charm; its scale and treatment are related to the Swiss cottage in the earlier book.

The forthright, exposed-construction members of the Alpine house appealed to Samuel H. Brooks, who created a series of designs for the middle class, with the purpose of equalizing their dwellings with the homes of the wealthy, "as regards essential comfort, convenience, and beauty." The assertion is made in his introduction to *Designs for Cottage and Villa Architecture*, London, [1840] (p. [iii]). His offerings vary from Greek to Gothic Revival and show Italian and Swiss influences. Several combine the last two rather strangely, with brick nogging or squared flint-stones filled between vertical timbers rising to large brackets supporting wide eaves. A porch and balcony adjoin the tower. Brooks was a carpenter at heart and included plates showing wood-joinery details isometrically. Except where the medieval houses become somewhat archaeological (in the use of half-timber walls and upper-story overhangs) and the Greek houses have towers, the types shown in *Cottage and Villa Architecture* relate more closely to buildings eventualized in the United States than in England; and American revival architecture favors Brooks's work better than that of any other British architectural writer.[23] If his work did nothing else, it accomplished greater acceptability for timber construction.

The book that more than any other set the taste for country places during the second half of the nineteenth century was John Claudius Loudon's *An Encyclopaedia of Cottage, Farm and Villa Architecture*,

Fig. 10

Fig. 11

THE AMERICAN BUNGALOW

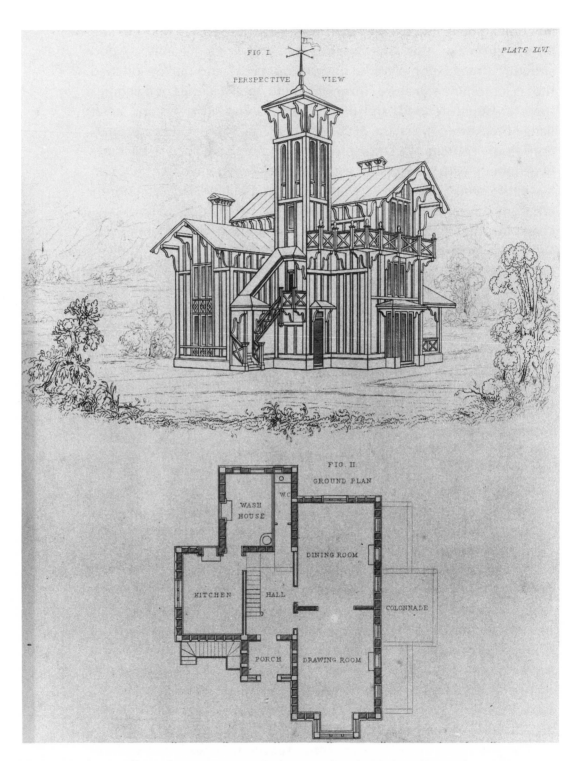

11. Design for a Villa in the Picturesque Style Prevailing in Various Parts of the Alps. S. W. Brooks, *Designs for Cottage and Villa Architecture*, London, [1840].

London, 1836. The 1,124-page volume is amply sprinkled with illustrations having to do with the residence, with its decoration, landscaping, useful dependencies, and garden ornaments, and includes house perspectives, elevations, and plans, alternative designs for aesthetic comparison, topography layouts, views and vistas, vignettes, diagrams of mechanical appliances and furniture. Few of the cuts showed graphic sensitivity, and the crowding of text and figures detracts from the appeal of either. The *Encyclopaedia* summarized and commented upon past accomplishments and included all sorts of modern conveniences, offering a precedent for just about anything anybody wanted to build; but one suspects that readers generally were more confused than edified by it all. The influence of Loudon's *Encyclopaedia* in America was indirect, through those elements adopted by and incorporated into the publications of Andrew J. Downing, whose work will be discussed in the following chapter.

From about 1860 to 1900 there was a movement in England known as the Domestic Revival. It strove to promote a sensible, comfortable style based upon conservative indigenous models from the late medieval era onward. The chief exponents were Philip Webb and Richard Norman Shaw, both born in 1831 and therefore coming into their prime at this time together. In 1859 Webb designed and built a house at Upton (now a suburb south of London) for poet–craftsman–artist William Morris. It was called Red House, and in the asymmetrical massing, steep roofs, picturesque chimneys, and pointed-arch details, the house was appropriately medieval and reflected Morris's source period of applied-arts inspiration. On the other hand, the clean-cut openings (some with sash windows) and the house's solid and spacious feeling were not period but derived from the architect's innate good sense of form orchestration. *Fig. 12* Although not a small building, Red House is without architectural pretentions.

R. Norman Shaw had more flair for complexity, as shown in his Leyes Wood (1868–69), Sussex, which is like a medieval manor on a mountain top. It is a pile embracing a walled courtyard, entered through a turreted gatehouse, the building proper having low masonry walls or high black-and-white overhangs pierced by compound casements and sheltered by elaborate bargeboarded gables, chimney uprights accented against the walls, and tall stacks penetrating steep, complicated roofs.[24] Shaw went on from here to a more personal style that gathered motifs from the early Renaissance. His own home (1875), Ellerdale Road,

12. The Red House, Upton, Kent. Philip Webb, Architect.
Drawn by the author.

Hampstead, London, is picturesque; but the mass of the four-storied brick building is essentially rectangular, weighted by towerlike chimneys, unequal bay-window tiers projecting near the extremities of the facade, a gable above each, with a variety of windows cut into the intervening flat surface.[25] Through the derivation of many of his motifs, the Shaw style has been called "Queen Anne." Its hallmark is the projecting window having bowed sides, and archivolt with open spandrels in the advanced plane describing a sort of Palladian opening. The Ellerdale Road house displays such a bay in front near the left flank. The "Queen Anne" in smaller houses was a reverting to the past, which, as we have noted, is a recurring Anglo-Saxon practice.

The first building in England to be designated a bungalow dates from 1869; and it has been characterized—as has the whole early bungalow movement in Britain, for that matter—as a "second home."[26] It was a low but not a small dwelling at the recently developed ocean-side resort of Westgate-by-the-Sea, just west of Margate and several miles from the Village of Birchington. A railroad had reached this area six years earlier, and a station was to be opened at Westgate in 1870. This prototype bungalow was rectangular, about 30 feet wide and almost three times as long, covered by a low-pitched roof with wide eaves supported on brackets. Its walls were constructed of prefabricated blocks, sustaining a roof system of unit timbers on which were laid patented roofing tiles. The model was advertised as a portable building, meaning that its parts could be assembled anywhere. The bungalow contained two large interiors, a drawing room and dining room, with sloping ceilings and large studio windows at one end, and fireplaces in a chimney between them. Adjoining was an entrance hall, which opened to a 60-foot-long corridor running through the middle of the house, covered by a sort of corbel vault, giving access to ten squarish rooms—a kitchen, library, six bedrooms, and two others that could be bedrooms or dressing rooms, all but the last two provided with corner fireplaces. Necessities flanked a lobby at the end, and a small lean-to on the side of the building, off the kitchen, housed a scullery and other service facilities. A basement accommodated storage. The architect, John Taylor, occupied such a bungalow, and some dozen others were built at Birchington, two of which were sold to such notables as the medic Erasmus Darwin and the painter–poet D. G. Rossetti. Taylor had a partner in J. P. Seddon, who owned the land there, and the architects also constructed along similar lines two-storied bungalows and the Bungalow Hotel nearby.[27] Besides unit structural members for buildings, John Taylor devised "chair furniture," whereby standard components could be assembled into various articles, such as chairs and tables, and "sanitary appliances," including damp-proof courses and ventilating devices. The first English bungalow was meant to be mass-produced, and as such it consummated the Industrial Revolution.

Fig. 13

Fig 14

The manifestation of the bungalow in England was irrevocably tied up with the Industrial Revolution. As suggested earlier, the first bungalows were second homes, seaside or seasonal cottages. The initial specimen (here illustrated) cost 1,800 guineas and therefore was out of reach for the working classes. But it was meant that they, too, should be provided with the means of getting away from the population centers, rendered congested, noisy, restless, smoky, and otherwise undesirable because of industrialization, and enabled to relax by the ocean or other unspoiled natural setting. The bungalow later would become a family's only home; and located in the suburbs it served as an out-of-town haven the year around. An architect, R. A. Briggs, built several bunga-

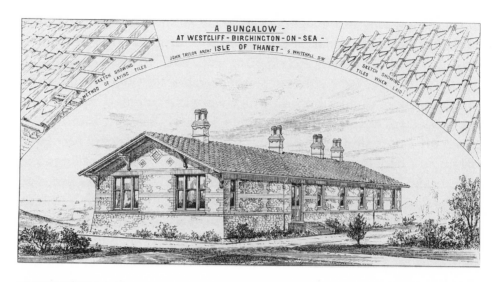

13. Perspective and Diagram of Wall Construction of the Bungalow at Westgate or Westcliff, Birchington. *Building News*, 15 August 1873.

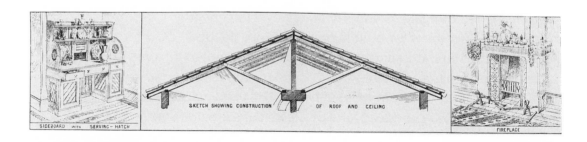

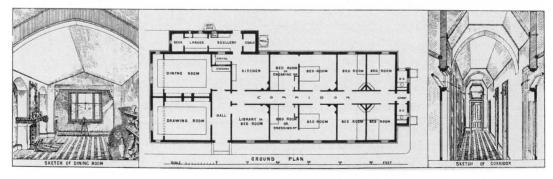

14. Diagram of Roof Construction, Interior Views and First-floor Plan of the Birchington Bungalow. *Building News*, 15 August 1873.

lows at East Grinstead, about thirty miles south of London, in 1887. The development was called Ballagio, whose ''surrounding country . . . [consisted of] fertile meadows on every side . . . with dark patches of woodland.'' Prospective clients were advised that this was ''decidedly the place to get to, for here in your bungalow, hidden away amongst wooded slopes, you can be lost to the outer world as completely as you wish.''[28] Briggs published a book of designs called *Bungalow and Country Residences* in 1891. In the fifth edition, 1901, the first plate illustrates an example that reflects the South Asian bungalow far more than had the severe Taylor house. Briggs's also is single-storied and has masonry walls, but the latter are of natural stone and stucco, and it has a thatched hipped roof and a recessed veranda at the entrance. Its plan is casual, with the hall having a fireplace inglenook in place of a formal drawing room, a dining room with projecting bay window (actually a small octago-

Fig. 15

15. Perspective and Plan for a Thatched Bungalow. R. A. Briggs, *Bungalows and Country Residences*, London, 1901.

THE AMERICAN BUNGALOW

16. Perspective and Plans for a Two-storied Bungalow.
Briggs, *Bungalows and Country Residences.*

nal corner turret), kitchen, servants' rooms, toilet facilities, and three bedrooms. There is no basement, and the garret could be used only for storage. The house has individuality and charm, and its main story is only a little more than half the size of Taylor's prototype at Birchington.

R. A. Briggs's bungalows are all picturesque, but most of them depart from any resemblance to the Indian namesake. In his book just cited, two of the "bungalow houses" have white stuccoed walls that rise to become curvilinear parapet gables, which are identified as having been taken from Boer houses in South Africa.[29] Another is a compact, two-storied clapboarded "bungalow." It has bracketed eaves, and the upper floor projects at either end, with an open "balcony" between, over the veranda across the front of the lower story. There are a hall, sitting room, and kitchen-scullery downstairs, and five bedrooms above, most with fireplaces. A Palladian window in one front gable seems somewhat

Fig. 16

out of character. It is difficult to see the building as a bungalow, but the author–architect defends the designation in the preface: ''A Bungalow in England has come to mean neither the sun-proof squat house of India, nor the rough log house of colder regions. It is not necessarily a one-story building, nor is it a country cottage. A Bungalow essentially is a little 'nook' or 'retreat.' A Cottage is a little house in the country, but a Bungalow is a little country house—a homey, cosy little place, with verandah and balconies and the plan so arranged as to ensure complete comfort, with a feeling of rusticity and ease. Cheapness and economy are important factors, but they should not be obtained at the cost of substantiality and utility.'' Briggs makes the point that it is more economical ''to have a house of two storeys'' than ''all the rooms on one floor,'' and ''the sanitary arrangements . . . must of course receive great attention, and . . . the most approved system must be adopted.'' One notes their limitations in his first design, and looks for them in vain in the second. The English fell far short of American plumbing standards at the beginning of and well into the present century.

Briggs's definition of a bungalow as a little country house or ''cosy'' retreat was capable of wide application. In all likelihood it was this flexibility that preserved the term in England, where it still persists in the vocabulary, applied to the ''small, cheap (and, by architects, generally looked-down-on) dwelling,'' and to little retirement homes, ''i.e., 'Grandma's bungalow' of the 1930s, as well as to lavish one-story suburban dwellings of today.''[30] The form (if not the bulk) has strayed far from that of the Indian caravanserai.

NOTES

1. Streynsham Master Manuscript: *Diary*.

2. Thornton: *English Pilot*, Vol. III, p. 54. *A New English Dictionary on Historical Principles*, Oxford, 1888, Vol. I, p. 1178.

3. Mrs. Sherwood, *The Lady of the Manor*, Bridgeport, Conn., 1828, Vol. V, p. 50. The first English edition, in seven volumes, was issued at Wellington between 1825 and 1829.

4. Vol. XXIV, no. 1704, 19 August 1908, p. 63.

5. ''The Origin of the Bungalow,'' *Country Life in America*, Vol. XIX, no. 8, February 1911, pp. 308–310.

6. *A New English Dictionary*, Vol. X, part II, p. 118.

7. Osvald Sirén, *China and Gardens of Europe of the Eighteenth Century*, New York, 1950, p. 107 ff.

8. Two more of the same title came out in 1797 and 1801; *Antiquities of India* appeared in 1797, *Views in Hindoostan* in 1801, and *Hindoo Excavations in the Mountain of Ellora* in 1803. A book of fifty

smaller plates, of which only five were of India, was Thomas and William Daniell's *A Picturesque Voyage to India, by Way of China*, 1810. A similar publication had been William Hodges's *Select Views in India, Drawn on the Spot, in the Year 1780, . . . 1783, and Executed in Aqua Tinta*, 1780. All were printed in London.

9. Christopher Hussey, ''Sezincote, Gloucestershire,'' *Country Life*, Vol. LXXXV, no. 2208, 13 May 1939, pp. 502–506; continued, *ibid.*, Vol. LXXXV, no. 2209, 20 May 1939, pp. 528–532. A photograph of the Indian bridge is reproduced on p. 530.

10. John N. Summerson, *John Nash*, London, 1935, p. 160.

11. H. Repton, *Designs for the Pavillion at Brighton*, London, [plates dated 1808].

12. Edward W. Brayley, *Illustrations of Her Majesty's Palace of Brighton*, London, 1838.

13. Thomas Daniell, *Oriental Scenery*, London, 1795, plate XXII.

14. *Ibid.*, plate XXIII.

15. That the bungalow type was clearly linked with India in the nineteenth century is shown by the Theodore Shillaker house in Honolulu, which was characterized as ''in the East Indian style'' when nearing completion (*The Polynesian*, 22 May 1847) and was identified as the ''Bungalow'' on the P. Emmert lithographic view of that community in 1854. Items submitted by Charles E. Peterson of Philadelphia. Illustrated on p. 10.

16. As in ''An Imperial Palace for Sovereigns of the British Empire,'' watercolor reproduced in black and white in John Summerson, *Heavenly Mansions*, New York, [1948], plate XXXIII.

17. *Ibid.*, Chapter V, ''The Vision of J. M. Gandy'' (pp.111–134), p. 116.

18. *Ibid.*, p. 114. This influence is more apparent in the first book, *Designs for Cottages*, than in the second.

19. See G. L. Medson, *On the Landscape Architecture of the Great Painters of Italy*, London, 1828.

20. Summerson, *John Nash*, illustrated plate III.

21. P. F. Robinson, *Rural Architecture*, London, 1823, plate 23.

22. *Ibid.*, plate 56.

23. Brook's *Designs* is not included in Downing's list of recommended books in *Landscape Gardening* (note p. 287), probably because the English book (published only the previous year) had not yet been discovered by the American. As will be seen in the following chapter, some influence seems likely in Downing's later books.

24. Bird's-eye view, reproduced in *Building News*, 31 March 1871.

25. Illustrated: Nikolaus Pevsner, *Pioneers of Modern Design*, New York, 1949, fig. 13, p. 34.

26. Anthony King, ''The Bungalow,'' part 2, *Architectural Association Quarterly*, vol. 5, no. 4, 1974, pp. 6–8.

27. *Ibid.*, p. 8, also note 9, p. 20.

28. R. A. Briggs, *Bungalows and Country Residences*, London, 1891, preface.

29. *Ibid.*, plates IV, VIII.

30. Letter from Anthony D. King, 28 January 1979. Dr. King's book, *The Bungalow: The Production of a Global Culture*, was published in 1984 by Routledge and Kegan Paul, London. See notes 26 and 27 above.

NATIVE ANTECEDENTS OF
THE AMERICAN BUNGALOW

THE BUNGALOW, for all its shorter life span in the United States, enjoyed as much patronage as in England, especially in the Western states, which, at the time, were still in the process of being settled. The first bungalows appeared soon after the Philadelphia Centennial (1876), initially in the East and then spread across the continent, and examples continued to be built up into the decade of the 1930s. The Centennial redirected the attention of the nation to the original ideals of freedom and proletarian simplicity, and after one hundred years of following the Old World stylistic precedent in architecture, the time had come to apply American principles in the building field, to stage an architectural revolution. The bungalow was the result of the overthrow of Eclecticism. Bungalow designers strove for straightforward solutions to the problems confronting them and became, therefore, pioneers. They broke new ground by choice, rather than physical necessity, yet they related to the colonists who settled on the Eastern Seaboard and the pioneers who penetrated inland. Constructions of the early and later settlers show traits in common, and whether derived one from the other or resulting from similarity of methods applied to corresponding conditions is of little moment. Being contradictory to the definition and ideals of the bungalow rules out obvious imitation; but earlier influences from the native soil were inevitable, and it will be the endeavor of this chapter to investigate them.

Seventeenth- and eighteenth-century American buildings most familiar to those who created bungalows were in New England. This was due to the recording expedition of architects McKim, Mead, Bigelow, and White to Newport, Marblehead, Salem, Newburyport, and Portsmouth in 1877, and certain publications that followed.[1] Examples investigated were of frame construction. The greater employment of brick in early Virginia and the South began to be investigated a decade later, but the more sophisticated architecture of the gentry in the Southern colonies had little that was adaptable to bungalow design.[2] The Pilgrims, who landed on Plymouth Rock in 1620, at first took the cue from their Indian hosts and constructed crude wigwams using bent saplings covered with

THE AMERICAN BUNGALOW

bark, adding their own convenience of a fireplace. As soon as conditions permitted they built permanent homes, which were fashioned after the modest houses they had known in England, whose type was a survival of late medieval rural. Because of more severe winters in Massachusetts, exposed half-timberwork was found impractical, and a covering of weatherboards was affixed to the wood frame. A huge masonry chimney in the center stabilized the framework and provided flues and fireplaces for the rooms. Buildings had no more magnitude or elaboration than required: ceilings were low to conserve heat; posts, beams, and joists were exposed; walls were plastered, sheathed in flush boards, or given rudimentary paneling; doors were mostly batten; leaded casement windows were small, as glass had to be imported, and they were set high for maximum light and ventilation; and floors were of random-width planks. All materials were innocent of paint or other applied finishes. It was a setting for the simple life. The family meeting place was the multiple-purpose hall or keeping room. As families increased and further accommodations were needed, dwellings ex-

Fig. 17   panded in an informal, asymmetrical manner.

Dutch settlers, in the Hudson River Valley and New Jersey, built

17. The Saltonstall House, Ipswich, Mass. Edwin Whitefield, *Homes of Our Forefathers in Massachusetts*, Boston, 1892. The far corner of the house (to the right of the chimney) was built *ca.* 1640, the balance of the two-storied front (left) in 1670. The rear lean-to (near side) was added in the eighteenth century.

18. Peter Lefferts House, Flatbush, N.Y. The original section was built in 1777, the larger addition (beyond) in the early nineteenth century. Photo 1967.

similarly to the English, but they used masonry (though stone more than brick) as much as the Southern colonists. With the Dutch came the Flemish, who had fled to Holland during the 1620s due to the Spanish invasion. Because of the scarcity of farms in the Lowlands, the Flemish moved on to America and set up farms on the western end of Long Island. Their houses were frame and had two unique features that were to become bungalow characteristics. The first is shingle siding, which by the end of the seventeenth century was taken over throughout the Northern English settlements, and the second is overhanging eaves. *Fig. 18* The roof projection, or "flying gutters," as the Flemish called them, came from the maritime region, which is now southern Holland, western Belgium, and the northern tip of France, where farmhouses had walls of clay mixed with lime and straw that had to be protected from rain. On Long Island the roof usually flared or curved outwardly, even after becoming double-pitched around 1700.[3] Later in the century the overhang became a porch, with a platform having, along the outer edge, a row of colonnettes supporting the roof.

For rusticity of effect, the use of exposed log walls surpassed shingle siding. Early English and Dutch colonists knew nothing about the house built of horizontal logs because it was nonexistent in their homelands. Such log construction belongs to wooded, mountainous regions, like Scandinavia and the European Alps. It was introduced to America by the Swedes, who settled Delaware in 1638. They built cabins of round logs notched to fit together at the corners, with protruding ends, and pegged into the upright frames of door and window openings. Fireplaces were of masonry, although the chimney above the throat may have been of sticks, coated with thick mud or clay inside to prevent its burning. The advantages of the log house were that it was built of the most readily available materials, with the simplest tools (the greatest amount of the work was performed with an ax), and, inasmuch as thick wood provides good insulation, the log house is cool in summer and can be made warm in winter. Germans pushing into Pennsylvania by way of the Delaware River were the second ethnic group to employ log construction. Next it was adopted by the Irish. Then the English took it up, and by the middle of the eighteenth century the log house had become the prevalent form of frontier shelter for settlers crossing the Alleghenies, as well as for new migrants to the coastal colonies. The later phase made use of squared logs, which were neatly fitted together, with overlapping, dovetailed, or saddle joints; and planks served for floors, partitions, and stairways.[4]

Fig. 19

European visitors are often struck by the prevalence of the open porch on American houses, even those of early vintage. We have seen that the Flemish developed it here late in the eighteenth century. It was as much used in New England at the same time; and it has an older heritage among the English in the South, going back to the seventeenth century.[5] But nowhere was the porch more in evidence than in French colonial architecture in the Mississippi Valley, often encircling the building. Another peculiarity here was the persistence of casement windows, which had been abandoned by other settlers at the beginning of the eighteenth century. The French, on the other hand, developed casements into *balcon-fenêtres*, or French doors, for shops fronting the street or chambers opening onto galleries. Often the chambers could be entered only from the gallery, which thus substituted for an enclosed passageway. Early dwellings had double-pitched hipped roofs, the steeper in the middle covering the house, and lower supplements extending over the galleries. Houses in the Illinois region were built of *poteaux-sur-sole* construction, consisting of upright squared timbers

19. Joseph B. Carroll House, Jessamine County, Ky. Photo by J. Winston Coleman II. The house was built in 1785. Originally an open dogtrot bisected the first story but had been partially filled in when this picture was made. Lower windows had been enlarged. The upper windows are modern.

set contiguous to one another on a wood sill resting on stone foundations, the visual effect of which was that of a log cabin upended. Perimeter posts sustained the gallery eaves. In the lower Mississippi Valley, due to soil saturation and occasional flooding, houses of like form were built upon a high basement, the first or main story being up one flight. They were the homes of the Spanish, who were ceded New Orleans and the territory west of it by the Treaty of Paris in 1763. They held the area until Napoleon wrested all Spanish possessions in 1801. The new French regime was short-lived, as the United States acquired the land between the Mississippi River and the Rocky Mountains through the Louisiana Purchase two years later. At the World's Columbian Exposition of 1893 in Chicago, the Louisiana exhibition was housed in a raised cottage styled after Creole plantation residences on the Bayou St. Jean north of the Crescent City. The American bungalow drew more features from the inland and southern French/Spanish type of house than any other yet considered.

The Spanish, pushing up from Mexico, explored the Southwest and California during the sixteenth century, as prelude to their establishing

Fig. 20

Fig. 21

THE AMERICAN BUNGALOW

20. French Residence at Cahokia, Ill. It was built *ca.* 1737 and after 1793 served as a courthouse. Taken to the St. Louis Fair in 1903, then to Jackson Park, Chicago, the parts were returned to Cahokia and reerected in 1939. Photo 1954.

21. The Louisiana State Building at the World's Columbia Exposition, Chicago, Ill. H. H. Bancroft, *The Book of the Fair*, Chicago, 1893.

missions and a colonial empire here a little later. Among all of the white invaders, they were unique in adopting an aboriginal mode of building, which was substantial and well-suited to the warm and arid climate. The model was the American Indian pueblo, or adobe community, whose form harks back at least to the tenth century. Pueblos were built by settled agrarians and served partly for protection against unfriendly nomads. They sometimes rose as many as five stories in receding terraces. Roofs were nearly flat, doors and windows few and small. Rooms of the first level usually were entered by ladder through a hole in the roof. The Spanish ignored the pueblo form, taking over only the adobe composition. Sun-hardened bricks were made of loam, sand, clay, straw, and tile chips or other binder. Wall surfaces were coated with mud and whitewashed with gypsum, becoming, in the course of time, a protective stucco. They were spanned by round logs, the ends of which sometimes projected beyond the building, and these carried smaller poles and a layer of rushes or split sticks as a base for the thick layer of roofing clay. Protruding spouts were provided to direct rainwater away from the vulnerable walls. This methodology was used for building great mission churches and small *hacienda* or *rancho* houses.[6] Surviving ranch houses in California date from the early-to-mid-nineteenth century. They are normally a one-story arrangement of rooms in alignment, flanked by a gallery, embracing two, three, or four sides of a courtyard or patio. There were glazed windows, some of the rooms had fireplaces, and sloping roofs were covered with shingles or tiles, thus showing some advancement over Indian habitations. The single-story *Fig. 22* layout and open court became bungalow ideals.

   The early Gallic-Latin houses on the North American continent suggest a counterpart that takes us afield to the Caribbean, to that tropic portion of the New World first mistaken by European explorers for parts of India, a false identity perpetuated in the designation "West Indies." Our example is an old farmhouse near Marianao, Cuba. Sketches of it were made by Boston bungalow-architect Julius Adolph Schweinfurth and published in 1907, including perspectives (only one here reproduced), plan, elevations, and details. Walls of the house are of adobe *Figs. 23, 24* thickness, and the principal rooms are aligned along a cross-axis, with a veranda across the entire front, and lesser rooms and a recessed porch in back. The roof and part of the flooring are tile, found similarly in the California *rancho*. The roof structure is double-pitched, the steeper portion over the house proper, as with French dwellings along the Missis-

THE AMERICAN BUNGALOW

22. Courtyard of the Ranch House of Don Pio Pico in California. D. R. Hannaford and R. Edwards, *Spanish Colonial or Adobe Architecture of California, 1800–1850*, New York, [1931].

sippi. The arrangement corresponds to that of the "very common form" of East Indian bungalow seen earlier, even to doors on axis, only the gallery does not carry around the ends of the Cuban house, and there is only one indented piazza at the rear. The Cuban *casa* is without clerestory, but none figured in early East Indian bungalows either. The parallels between the Indian caravanserai, Caribbean farmhouse, and French and Spanish colonial houses in North America stem principally from basic requirements common to all.

Fig. 3

Fig. 1

With the establishment of the United States government at the beginning of the fourth quarter of the eighteenth century, the nation between the Atlantic coast and Mississippi River thereafter favored English culture, and the accepted mode of architecture, known as Federal, was a continuation of the Georgian style. Academically oriented amateur architects, such as Thomas Jefferson and Dr. William Thornton, and the newly emerging professionals, including Charles Bulfinch, Samuel McIntire, Asher Benjamin, Benjamin Henry Latrobe, and their followers propagated classicism, and prepared the scene for the formal Greek Revival. Latrobe, in fact, effected the change. Soon after his arrival from England he introduced the Greek orders in his design for the Bank of Pennsylvania (1798) in Philadelphia.[7] The Greek Revival embodied other characteristics differentiating it from the Federal, such as masculinity, bigness of form, spaciousness, and an adherence to rectangularity in openings. The Fed-

23. Perspectives of Farm House near Marianao, Cuba. Drawings by J. A. Schweinfurth. *American Architect and Building News*, 28 December 1907.

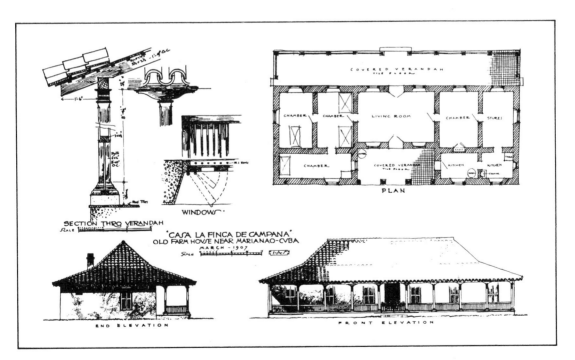

24. Front Elevation and Details of the Farm House near Marianao, Cuba. Measured Drawings by J. A. Schweinfurth. *American Architect and Building News*, 28 December 1907.

eral and Greek Revival styles were alike in that their builders looked for guidance to the architectural handbooks of the period, such as those of Benjamin (mentioned as an architect above) for the first, and those of Minard Lafever for the latter.[8] These builder's guides concentrated on the orders and proper elevations of house features, primarily doorways and fireplaces, with diagrams on construction and occasional floor plans. The Greek Revival was more prevalent here than in England (which tended to adhere to the Palladian Classic), and from the 1820s to the outbreak of the Civil War it virtually served as the national American style.

The classic upsurge naturally was accompanied by a romantic re-action, predominantly Gothic Revival, which was just as much beholden to European—especially English—medieval antecedents as the Greek Revival was to ancient Hellenic models. The romantic architectural styles were promoted by books as was its counterpart, only they were of different character. These were house-pattern books, in which orders were abandoned and elevations minimized in favor of perspective sketches of dwellings in their settings, and floor plans, with some few details, and interiors and furnishings. The nature of builder's guides had been to stifle architectural freedom, even though Lafever presented some of his own original orders.[9] Although wearing a new guise, they were restrictive orders nevertheless, a retention of old forms, only changed in details. The later house-pattern books offered greater diversity, some designs being based upon historic types not generally followed at that time, and others were especially devised for the sort of reader who would be purchasing the book, suitable to his needs, his pocketbook, and offering some degree of hominess and aesthetic appeal. The change came around 1840.

A transitional work—without orders and therefore no builder's guide, yet not showing house perspectives in landscape and hence no fully developed house-pattern book either—was John Hall's *A Series of Select and Original Modern Designs*, Baltimore, 1840. The title is reminiscent of Minard Lafever's *The Beauties of Modern Architecture*, issued five years earlier, only the combined words "original" and "design" have a creative implication at variance with the more stilted term "architecture," which is indicative of the book's contents. It is significant, too, that the place of publication is not New York City but Baltimore, not the high megapolis of decorum but a Southern community, setting of an easier way of life and more casual building. The house design chosen for

NATIVE ANTECEDENTS

THE AMERICAN BUNGALOW

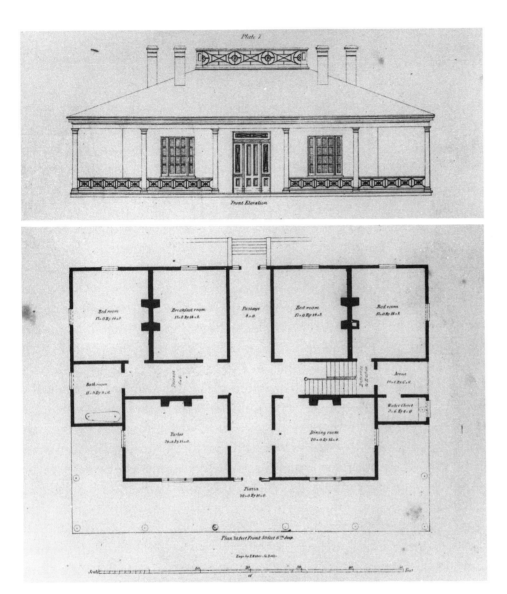

25. Front Elevation and Plan for a One-story Cottage with a
Basement and Other Conveniences. John Hall, *A Series of Select
and Original Modern Designs*, Baltimore, 1840.

inclusion here has older Dixie characteristics, propagated by a warm
climate and layout developed for entertaining. Plate 7 represents a low-
slung residence with truncated hipped roof and a ten-foot-wide piazza
half encircling it. Railings around the roof platform and between the
plain Tuscan columns of the piazza are of lattice design, a favorite motif

Fig. 25

in the buildings of Thomas Jefferson. The accompanying description recommends masonry foundations and wood frame for the super-structure, save for brick walls flanking the two rear chimneys. The form recalls that of the French house in the Mississippi Valley, which, in 1840, still was being built in the Deep South as the raised cottage. In the design by Hall the main story is closer to the ground, although the kitchen is in the basement, accessible by an inside stairway and outside steps under the back stoop. Rooms of the main story are arranged about a cruciform hall, the parlor and dining room balancing one another at the front; three bedrooms and a breakfast room are behind; and a bath is at one end of the cross hall, a water closet at the other off an open "arrea." Adjoining it, in the cross passage, a staircase ascends to the garret, which is lighted by a "lantern-dome" within the roof railing. The claim to this concept's being an "original modern design" is justified, first, in the matter of easy circulation, and, second (remembering that this was 1840), in that the orders have been reduced to maximum sim-plicity and minimum supporting potency. It forms a link between the early galleried house and the later bungalow.

By far the most influential writer in the field of American house-building during the romantic period was Andrew Jackson Downing. As stated in the preceding chapter, Downing was influenced by the work of John Loudon. His books offered house designs for the country set-ting in Gothic, both cottage and castellated, Romanesque or Norman, Anglo-Italian and Italian-villa types, and bracketed. The assortment of styles used by the romantics made a clean break with the classicists' practice of adhering strictly to prescribed forms. It tended to nullify the importance of style and lead to stylelessness—to spontaneity, or the natu-ral way of building—which sometimes was referred to as the "American" style, as in some of Alexander Jackson Davis's designs made for exhibi-tion.[10]

A. J. Downing was primarily a horticulturist, but the home require-ment forced him to expound (not unwillingly) on architecture. His first important book was *A Treatise on the Theory and Practice of Landscape Gardening*, New York, 1841, in which Section IX was devoted to "Land-scape or Rural Architecture" (pp. 269–347). Downing, more than any-body else, broke the reverence for formal balance and square forms in American residences. The section in *Landscape Gardening* is illustrated with a few cottages, villas, and manors composed asymmetrically, includ-ing Sunnyside, the stepped-gable snuggery of Washington Irving near

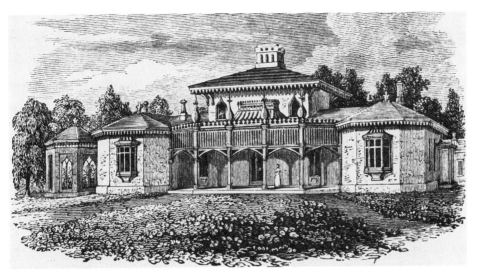

26. Residence of Nathan Dunn, Mount Holly, N.J. A.J. Downing, *A Treatise on the Theory and Practice of Landscape Gardening*, New York, 1841.

Tarrytown, before that house acquired its "pagoda" addition.[11] Some of the homes are of ample scale, such as the residence of Bishop Duane, Burlington, New Jersey, of which both perspective and first floor plan are given.[12] It is America's first Italian villa. A spreading house in bilateral balance, whose long veranda and wide eaves anticipate the bungalow is the seat of Nathan Dunn at Mount Holly. The building is described in Downing's text as a "semi-oriental" cottage; it may be compared to a design for "A Chinese Residence" in the English book that included a number of Eastern specimens, Richard Brown's *Domestic Architecture*.[13] Unlike his British counterpart, Downing did not find the Oriental a suitable model for New World homes, and indeed the exotic elements are played down in the Mount Holly house (as they are exaggerated in Brown's design), yet the architect of the Dunn house, John Notman of Philadelphia, receives, along with A. J. Davis of New York, the author's endorsement as "the most successful American architects in this branch of art."[14]

Fig. 26

Soon after *Landscape Gardening* Downing published a full-blown house-pattern book called *Cottage Residences* (New York, 1842), which included ten original house designs illustrated by perspective sketches and first- and second-floor plans. However, the title underrates the examples, which range up to Italian villas and castellated manors. The

27. Sketch and First-floor Plan of a Cottage Villa Constructed of Wood. A. J. Downing, *Cottage Residences*, New York, 1842.

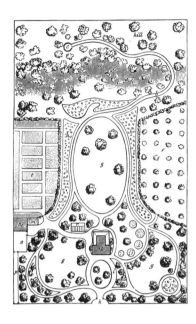

28. Plot Plan for Cottage, Design V. Downing, *Cottage Residences*, facing p. 98. Legend: *a*—steep hill, *b*—walk, *c*—summerhouse, *d*—residence, *e*—kitchen garden, *f*—orchard, *g*—lawn, *h*—flower borders, *j*—dahlia beds, *k*—entrance, *l*—carriage road, *m*—carriage house, *n*—barn and stable, *o*—stable yard, *p*—public road, *r*—greenhouse.

simplest in the collection is a two-storied, T-shaped house of vertical-board walls and deep bracketed eaves; a veranda envelops the three exposed sides of the rear wing. Concerning the construction system, Downing comments that "wood is acknowledged by all architects to be the worst material for building."[15] As an American house, the magnitude needs no apology: on the first floor it has a porch and entry in front of a central stairhall, large drawing room to one side and oblong dining room to the other, a water closet off a passage, and a bedroom and boudoir in the ell; a kitchen and three other rooms are in the basement; and five bedrooms are in the full second story. A masonry version, with slight plan variations, is included in *Cottage Residences*; but in spite of Downing's apology for wood, he chose the timber example to amplify the second edition of *Landscape Gardening*, which appeared in 1844. It was assumed the more suitable for American requirements, and the text informs us that the design partakes "somewhat of Italian and Swiss features."[16] Most of the houses depicted in *Cottage Residences* include their setting by means of a plot plan. The one here chosen was to be situated on two acres, which were level except for a rise at the back topped by a summerhouse. Interlaying it and the house are an elliptical lawn flanked by the kitchen garden and fruit orchard, the first bordered by flower beds, and the latter two enclosed by privet hedges. A greenhouse and dependencies are between

Fig. 27

Fig. 28

the house and kitchen garden, and driveways and walks meander through the premises.

The style of the building just seen was reflected in about the first third of the thirty-two schemes for residences in Downing's most influential tome, *The Architecture of Country Houses*, New York, 1850, whose ninth printing was issued in 1866. The first design, "A Small Cottage for a Working-man," is rectangular, covered by a simple roof with projecting eaves on exposed rafters, and having bracketed hoods sheltering doors and windows. It contains a stairway in the passage and two rooms on the first floor, and two others in the half story above. The second design is asymmetrical and has three chambers upstairs. Design III, although perfectly balanced, has a more homey look, with benches flanking the front door, their backs curving up and out, becoming great brackets supporting the little gabled overhang with triple windows to a *Fig. 29* small upper bedroom. The accommodations are similar to those of the house described from *Cottage Residences*, though the kitchen has been brought up from the cellar. Lack of veranda and balconies, and beam ends supporting eaves in place of brackets, make for a more forthright building design. Note, also, the innovation of vines climbing on the house itself, which took a horticulturist to devise, as no architect up to this time would have allowed it.

Another specimen in *Country Houses* worth our notice is Design *Fig. 30* VIII, a "Regular Bracketed Cottage." Downing distinguishes its "regularity" as something distinct from "symmetry," stating that the two halves of any side are not of "equal portions." Perhaps this is hairsplitting, and in the same vein he calls the house a "parallelogram" rather than a rectangle. As in earlier examples in the book there are overhanging eaves and window hoods, all of them supported on brackets projecting from the walls. This is a touch Downing identifies as "Picturesque," defined as a "manifestation of Beauty through *power*," the last word referring to a structural member elaborated visually.[17] The remarkable feature of the house is its use of an arbor-veranda along three sides, which, Downing points out, would be considerably less expensive than a roofed porch, and on which he recommended training grape vines (the "Isabella" or "Catawba"), providing both shade and edible fruit, and requiring little maintenance. Besides three rooms on the first floor, the kitchen, wash- and store-rooms are in the basement, and five bedrooms on the second floor range in size from 7-by-10 to 14-by-14 feet.

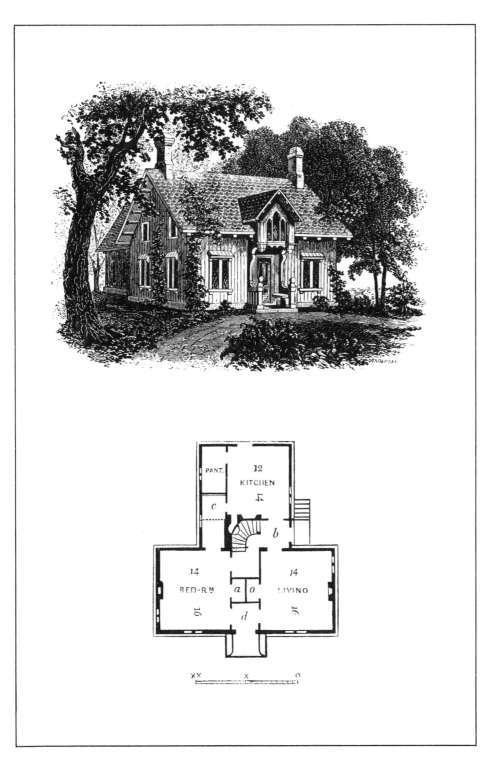

29. Perspective and First-floor Plan of a Symmetrical Bracketed Cottage.
A. J. Downing, *The Architecture of Country Houses*, New York, 1850.

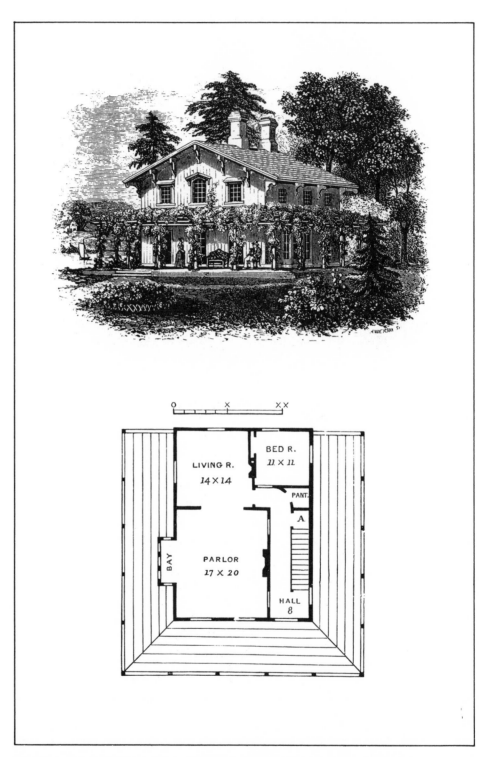

30. Perspective and First-floor Plan of a Regular Bracketed Cottage. Downing, *The Architecture of Country Houses*.

Design X culminates the Alpine style hinted at in earlier offerings in *Country Houses*. "The genuine Swiss cottage may be considered the most picturesque of all dwellings built of wood," Downing affirms; "it seems especially adapted to the wild and romantic scenery where it originated." He goes on to say: "The expression of the Swiss cottage is highly domestic, as it abounds in gables, balconies, large windows, and other features indicative of home comforts." However, Downing recognizes that there is no point "in our copying a Swiss chalet," as we would only perpetuate "all its defects." Also to be remembered is "that its peculiarities and picturesqueness must either be greatly modified to suit a tame landscape, or, if preserved, then a scene or locality should be selected which is in harmony with the style." The "Swiss cottage" shown had been designed by G. J. Penchard, an architect of Albany, and it was built as a tenant's cottage at Mount Hope, the estate of E. P. Prentice a mile below the city.[18] The roof of this Hudson River house is double-pitched (like French dwellings in the Mississippi River Valley) and jerkin-headed at the apex. Set on a battered podium of cobblestones, the walls above are articulated by a system of vertical and horizontal timbers anticipating the late-nineteenth-century "Stick Style."[19] Into this rectangular framework are set doors, windows, or panels shingled in an ornamental way. The last is hardly Swiss in origin; Downing admits it derived from "shingle-covered Dutch farm-houses in our vicinity" (he lived down-river at Newburgh).[20] Kitchen, service rooms, and a water closet are in the basement. Of the three large and two small rooms on the first floor, the second in importance, labeled "LIVING R.," is less formal than the parlor and was meant to be used for dining. Three good-sized bedrooms and a couple of closets are on the second floor. It is significant that this "chalet" was built during the 1840s and was not merely a dream in a plan book.

A. J. Downing gives nine more designs for bracketed residences in *The Architecture of Country Houses*; then he presents a dozen stylish villas in Romanesque, Italian, Classical, Pointed or Rural Gothic, and the more sophisticated English Tudor manners.

Charles Wyllys Elliott stressed the national characteristics of the designs in his book called *Cottages and Cottage Life, Containing Plans of Country Houses, Adapted to the Means and Wants of the People of the United States*, Cincinnati and New York, 1848. Examples included Gothic Revival cottages and Italian villas but also more casual types, befitting the subtitle. Our choice, as in the later Downing book, is of a

Fig. 31

Fig. 32

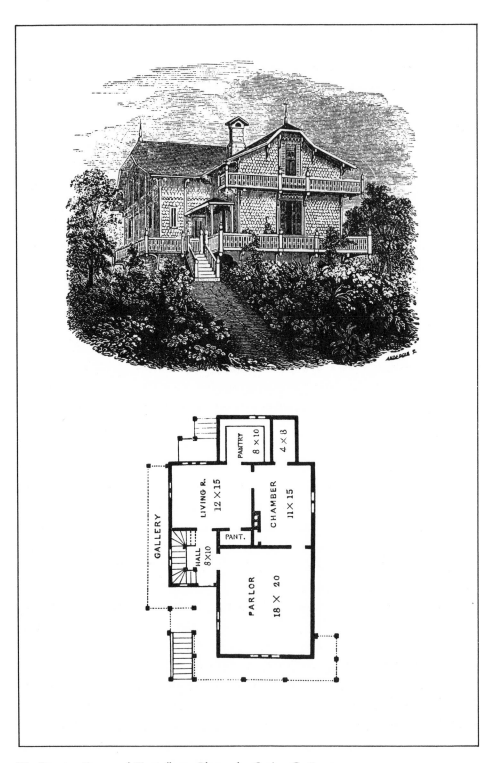

31. Perspective and First-floor Plan of a Swiss Cottage.
Downing, *The Architecture of Country Houses.*

constructed house. The lithographic view is of Frederick Tudor's house at Nahant, Massachusetts, a spreading building with extensions, having low-pitched gabled roofs, and perimeter galleries supported on slender posts. The composition suggests that parts have been later additions. *Fig. 33* Picturesque elements are its stone walls, hood molds over casement windows, brackets to the eaves, and the roof covered with bark. Elliott admits that the floor plan is his own invention, fabricated some time after visiting the house. A century later the Tudor residence at Nahant was serving as a clubhouse, and, although it had been altered and enlarged, clearly showed that a living hall always had occupied the front half of the main block, instead of having a central passage with rooms to either side. This is an important feature, as regards the later bungalow. We are informed by A. J. Downing that Frederick Tudor was "well known in the four quarters of the world, as the originator of the present successful mode of shipping ice to the most distant tropical countries."[21] From this we can speculate over what exotic influences from his commercial ventures were felt in the Nahant house. A Gulf Coast or Caribbean origin for the gallery seems not unlikely.

Many book titles of the mid-nineteenth century sound promising for our theme yet prove, upon examination, to be irrelevant. For instance,

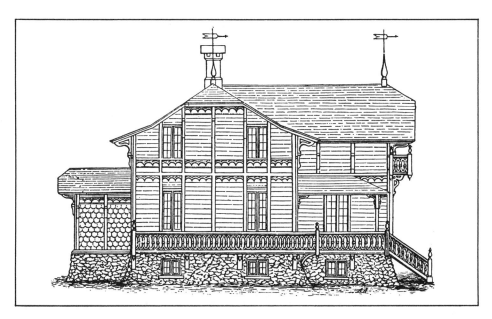

32. Right Flank Elevation of the Swiss Cottage. Downing, *The Architecture of Country Houses*.

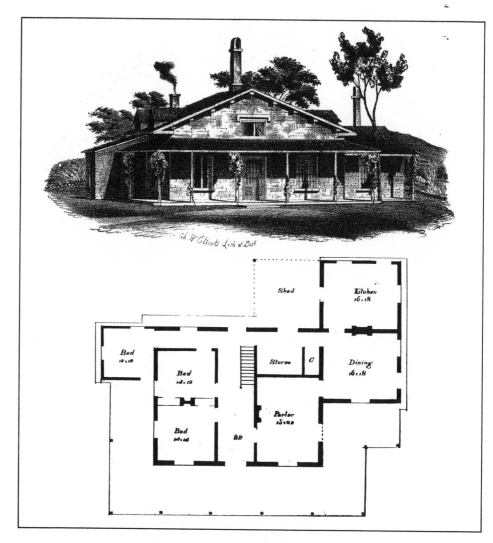

33. Sketch and First-floor Plan of Frederick Tudor's House at Nahant, Mass.
C. W. Elliott, *Cottages and Cottage Life*, Cincinnati and New York, 1848.

T. Thomas II's *The Working-man's Cottage Architecture*, New York, 1848,
containing plans and elevations for eleven little dwellings of from four
to eight rooms, costing from $225 to $1,080, is a catalog of pilastered,
pedimented, parapeted, bargeboarded, and crenellated designs, which,
if they lacked chimneys, might be mistaken for mausoleums.

The other extreme is the rustic shelter, exemplified in the log house.
With its early prevalence in this country, it seems odd that there was
not a continuation of the type (other than on the westward-moving

frontier), or more of a revival in the middle of the nineteenth century. One might expect log designs in Elliott's book of houses "Adapted to the Means and Wants of the People of the United States," but is disappointed. Calvert Vaux inserts a sketch and plan for one as a vignette in *Villas and Cottages.*[22] An interesting specimen appears in Charles P. Dwyer's *The Economic Cottage Builder*, published at Buffalo, New York, Boston, Philadelphia, Cincinnati, and Detroit, 1855. The first plate illustrates a "primitive dwelling of a backwoodsman as it might be made with but a trifling attention to details."[23] The cabin has walls of horizontal logs that overlap but are not notched together, an articulated center chimney, overhanging eaves and vertical boards in the gable, a projecting bay window at one end, and a wing opposite containing a "scullery" back of a recess. The author feels that the interior arrange-

Fig. 34

Fig. 35

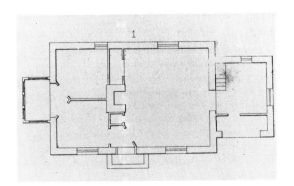

34, 35. Perspective Sketch and Floor Plan for a Log House. C. P. Dwyer, *Economic Cottage Builder*, Buffalo, 1855.

ments of most log houses call for improvement. In his version the general room occupies more than half of the main pavilion, with closets to either side of the fireplace, and the balance is divided into two bedrooms that have splayed corners whereby they share the bay window. With most of the building materials obtainable from or near the site, labor constituted the primary expenditure, which was estimated to be about $50.

There are two other designs in the *Economic Cottage Builder* deserving of a few words. The second plate is of a symmetrical house with walls of vertical logs, pointed-topped openings, and a complex hipped roof. The building is on a raised platform and contains polygonal rooms, for which the upright timbers are well suited. Plate Ten is of a plank-on-edge cottage with open porch on three sides, a smaller version of John Hall's house for the South. The Dwyer abbreviation was estimated to cost from $175 to $300.

Fig. 25

The factor that all of these American houses from the seventeenth to the mid-nineteenth century have in common, whether built by newly arrived English or Europeans, or by those born in the New World, and whether of log, frame, stone, or brick construction, is their rural environment, their integration with nature. The houses illustrated in books were shown usually in perspective, and those in the picturesque manner invariably were in an appropriate landscape setting. In the early

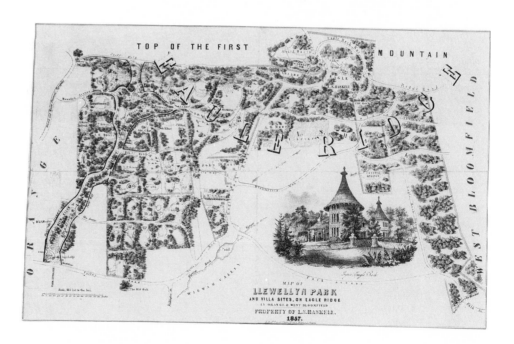

36. Map of Llewellyn Park, Orange, N.J., Lithograph, 1857. The Metropolitan Museum of Art, Harris Brisbane Dick Fund.

A. J. Downing volumes a plan for the grounds was given. All of these places were considered isolated retreats; and only after Downing's untimely decease did an aggregate of them come into existence. Beginning in 1852, Llewellyn P. Haskell collaborated with Alexander Jackson Davis, architect of many designs appearing in the Downing books, to fabricate a suburban development in the foothills of the Orange Mountains in New Jersey. It was called Llewellyn Park. The natural features of meadows, dells, woodlands, brooks, etc., were enhanced by the judicious placing of arbors, summerhouses, gazebos, and rustic bridges, and the various parts were made accessible by winding drives sympathetic to the contours of the countryside. Residential lots were of irregular shape and sufficiently large to provide personal privacy. Dwellings were built in the quaint styles provided by that period. Included were homes for Haskell himself, a rustic house on Eagle Rock called "Eyrie," and for Davis a compact Gothic villa entitled "Wildmont." Llewellyn Park was one of the great monuments to Romanticism in the United States. Of its architectural accents, only one original cottage and the circular gatehouse survive today.[24]

Fig. 28

Fig. 36

The direct descendant of Llewellyn Park is Tuxedo Park, in the Catskill Mountains about thirty miles northwest of New York City. It was the estate of tobacco magnate Pierre Lorillard, whose original idea was to keep it a hunting reservation where he and a few friends might put up little cottages, which Lorillard designated "boxes." The precinct was laid out as picturesquely as Haskell's in New Jersey. Then society took hold of the development, and the corrupted aboriginal place-name "Tuxedo" came to signify a gentleman's black-and-white formal dress. The rustic clubhouse was a sizable social center containing an octagonal ballroom and a hundred guest rooms. For years the New York social season was opened by the Debutantes' Ball in this building. It, the gatehouse, and forty informal cottages were designed by the architect Bruce Price and built during the early 1880s. One, situated on a hill beyond the clubhouse, was constructed for Addison Canmack and was called the Japanese Cottage.[25] Lower walls of the telescoped complex form are of stone. The half-timbered second story displays large Japanese crests in wood against plastered panels, and there are shingled gable ends. Eaves are slightly upturned at the corners, and pent roofs form deep overhangs at the base of each gable; a small entrance porch repeats the motif. The direct source of inspiration for this house would have been the exhibition building from the Island Empire at the Philadel-

Fig. 37

37. The Japanese Cottage at Tuxedo Park, N.Y. Bruce Price, Architect. "Great American Architects Series," No. 5, *Architectural Record*, June 1899.

Fig. 39   phia Centennial, of which the porch is a near duplicate. Note also its pent roofs. The style of the Canmack cottage was suitable to its setting, and its exoticism gave it snob appeal sufficient for Tuxedo Park.

With regard to exotic influences in late-nineteenth-century American architecture, mention should be made that in the first issue of the periodical *American Architect* (1876) exterior and interior sketches and a floor plan of a Chinese residence were reproduced. They accompanied and initiated a series of articles by Viollet-le-Duc on "The Habitations of Man in All Ages." Identified as "Fat Fau's House" and situated on the shore of a lake (with boat landing adjoining an overhanging wing), it is a

Fig. 38   compact cruciform composition of frame set on stone foundations. Gabled roofs are convex in the center and dipping at the eaves. A small portico precedes a front porch spanning the elevated main pavilion, with lower wings balanced right and left, an ell on axis behind, and a semidetached extension off to the side opposite the water. The high center room is lighted by clerestory windows in front and rear gables. Much of the construction was of bamboo, including the porch posts, which were joined by lattice railings of more slender members. Features here presented figured on later houses in or near Newport, Rhode Island, such as the imitation bamboo posts on Stanford White's Isaac

Bell house (1882–83), and a flightlike curvilinear roof over the projecting entrance to the John C. Bancroft house (1893).[26]

In the middle and latter half of the nineteenth century there was considerable consciousness of living with nature. Downing's ideal was for permanent abode (as with the Chinese), whereas Lorillard's favored seasonal residence. We are reminded of the English "second home" movement, discussed in the previous chapter, in whose fertile seedbed the first bungalow sprouted. The United States nurtured an equivalent movement that was equally widespread. It began at mid century, when

38. The Japanese Exhibition Building at the Philadelphia Centennial. Thomas Westcott, *Centennial Portfolio*, Philadelphia, 1876.

39. Fat Fau's House. *American Architect and Building News*, 26 February 1876.

THE AMERICAN BUNGALOW

40. Cottage at Nahant, Mass., Remodeled by Putnam and Tilden, 1872. Portfolio Club, *The Sketch Book*, Boston, 1873, No. VI.

vacationing Americans started to drift away from inland watering places to the seashore. Interrupted by the Civil War, the movement accelerated rapidly afterward. Early visitors to the Atlantic Ocean stayed at inns similar to those that had accommodated them in the mountains; but by the early 1870s a noticeable percentage began renting, buying, or building vacation homes, which invariably were called "cottages." Some were older houses refurbished to the tastes of the new owners. One such example was at Nahant, Massachusetts, extravagantly remodeled *Fig. 40* by Bostonians J. P. Putnam and George T. Tilden. The plain early dwelling was stifled under overpowering dormers, wide gables (secured from blowing away by iron rods), and a new veranda screened by lacelike lattices and frivolous cutout decorative motifs. Except for following some of the contours of the old house, the innovations were more ornamental than architectural.

Along the Eastern Seashore seasonal communities sprang up containing hundreds of lots, which were sold either with newly built houses on them or empty. They were known popularly as "Cottage Cities." John C. Bancroft was a trustee of the Land Trust Cottages that sponsored the Easton's Point development at Middletown, Rhode Island, laid out by Frederick Law Olmsted during 1885–87.[27] Perhaps the best known is Oak Bluffs on Martha's Vineyard. Excursion boats from the mainland ran to it regularly in season. Many of its cottages emulated the fancifulness of that just seen at Nahant. On the neighboring island of Nantucket, dozens of cottage cities were laid out during the 1870s and 1880s. One of the most ambitious was at the west end, covering a thousand acres, and with 2½ miles of ocean front from Great Neck to Smith's Point. Its 1,800 lots were made accessible by curving drives following the outlines of coves, ponds, and other preexisting features. The layout was promoted by the Nantucket Sea Shore Enterprise, headed by S. D. Tourtellotte of Worcester. Announcement was made that a hotel and a few cottages were to be ready by the spring of 1873. But Nantucket was too remote, too prudish (natives frowned upon drinking, scanty clothing on the beach, and off-islanders in general), and the endeavor was a fizzle; few lots were sold, no buildings were erected, and today about half of the site is inundated by the ocean, Smith's Point having become Smith's Island.[28]

Fig. 41

However, seaside cottages were built on Nantucket during the late nineteenth century. They were simple affairs, in a measure due to conscious imitation of old fishing shacks in the ancient village of Siasconset. A New York promoter, Edward F. Underhill, was captivated by Siasconset, delved into its history and traditions, and wrote a number of books and articles about it.[29] Underhill bought a few existing structures and spon-

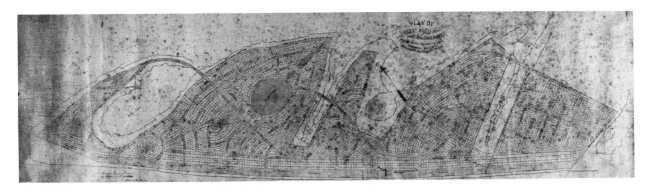

41. Plan of Great Neck and Smith's Point Cottage Lots. Cherrington and Marble, and A. J. Marble, Designers, Worcester, Mass., 1873. Nantucket Register of Deeds.

THE AMERICAN BUNGALOW

42. Furnished Seaside Cottages, Advertisement of Edward F. Underhill. *Inquirer and Mirror*, 21 May 1894.

43. Portable Houses for All Countries, Advertisement of the Portable House and Manufacturing Company, New York. *American Architect and Building News*, 6 October 1883.

sored the building of many more, and he rented them furnished to summer guests. His advertisement here reproduced gives thumbnail *Fig. 42* sketches of the quaint "patchwork" village and of his cottage offerings.

One other type of building should be looked into as an American antecedent to the bungalow. This is the portable structure, manufactured in the United States since at least mid century.[30] By the early 1880s the phenomenon had become sizable, composed of several stories and fulfilling many uses, as temporary and permanent shelters—rural, industrial, institutional, and residential. The Portable House and Manufacturing Company, 335 Broadway, New York City, supplied all parts, finished and painted, ready to assemble. Its advertisement showed the perspective of a "Summer Pavilion" of chateau proportions, and plans and elevations of a multistoried "Sea Side Cottage" with circumference verandas. This prefab relates to the first bungalow erected on British soil, made locally, and to an equivalent one that went there from the New World a few years later.

Fig. 43

Figs. 13, 55

NOTES

1. In 1858 Nathan Henry Chamberlain had read "A Paper on New-England Architecture" before the New-England Genealogical Society, which was published within the year as a 30-page pamphlet by Crosby, Nichols and Co., Boston, but it appeared in print without illustrations, thus lacking effectiveness. Arthur Little's *Early New England Interiors . . . Salem, Marblehead, Portsmouth and Kittery*, Boston, 1878, reproduced pen drawings of rooms, details, and staircases from houses on the McKim, Mead, Bigelow, and White route. Edwin Whitefield's multivolume, *The Homes of Our Forefathers . . .*, Reading, Mass., 1879–1889, presented tinted perspective sketches of houses in Maine, New Hampshire, Vermont, Massachusetts, Rhode Island, and Connecticut. The weekly *American Architect and Building News* first was published at Boston in 1876, and, beginning in Volume II, with "Georgian Houses of New England" (20 October 1877, pp. 338–339), regularly offered materials on early building in America.

2. Frank Edwin Wallis, *Old Colonial Architecture and Furniture*, Boston, *ca.* 1887, included sketches of several Southern interiors, such as Carter's Grove on the James River, and the Hammond-Harwood house in Annapolis. Joseph Everett Chandler's *The Colonial Architecture of Maryland, Pennsylvania and Virginia*, Boston, 1892, reproduced photographs of man-

sions, both outside and in, and a few public buildings.

3. As in the Nicholas Schenck house (*ca.* 1755), Brooklyn, N. Y., the first-floor interiors of which have been installed in the Brooklyn Museum. Marvin D. Schwartz, *American Interiors, 1675–1885*, Brooklyn, 1968, pp. [69]–77.

4. Harold R. Shurtleff, *The Log Cabin Myth*, Cambridge, 1939, Chapter VII, "Origin and Spread of the Log House," pp. [163]–185.

5. As at Bond Castle, Calvert County, and Birmingham Manor, Anne Arundel County, Maryland. Henry Chandlee Forman, *The Architecture of the Old South*, Cambridge, Mass., pp. 136–[137], 148–[149].

6. See Rexford Newcomb, *Old Mission Churches and Historic Houses of California*, Philadelphia, 1926; also D. R. Hannaford and R. Edward, *Spanish Colonial or Adobe Architecture in California, 1800–1850*, New York, 1931.

7. Talbot Hamlin, *Benjamin Henry Latrobe*, New York, 1955, pp. 152–157.

8. Of his six books (issued in 45 editions or printings), Asher Benjamin is best known for *The American Builder's Companion*, Boston, 1806, and *The Practical House Carpenter*, Boston, 1830. Of Minard Lafever's five books (13 editions or printings) the most influential were *The Modern Builder's Guide*, New York, 1833,

and *The Beauties of Modern Architecture*, New York, 1835.

9. Such as the "Corinthian" order, with gadrooning at the top of the campaniform, plate II, *The Beauties of Modern Architecture*. This unique form was employed in the three-storied columns of the Alabama State Capitol (1850–51), Montgomery.

10. In an exhibition drawing, dated 1835, the term is applied to an irregular villa labeled, in full, "Etruscan or American Style." Another (1848), a squarish, bracketed design with first-story encircling piazza, is called an "American Farm House." They are illustrated in Roger Hale Newton, *Town & Davis, Architects*, New York, 1942, plates 23, 22.

11. A. J. Downing, *Landscape Gardening*, New York, 1841, fig. 37, p. 325.

12. *Ibid.*, plate XLIII.

13. Clay Lancaster, "Oriental Forms in American Architecture, 1800–1870," *The Art Bulletin*, Vol. XXIX, no. 3, September 1947, figs. 25–26, pp. 192–193.

14. Downing, *Landscape Gardening*, note p. 347.

15. A. J. Downing, *Cottage Residences*, New York, 1842, p. 16 (p. 7 in 1847 edition).

16. Downing, *Landscape Gardening*, 2nd edition, 1844, p. 363.

17. A. J. Downing, *The Architecture of Country Houses*, New York, 1850, pp. 112–113.

18. *Ibid.*, pp. 123–124.

19. This rectangular framing can be traced to picturesque Alpine villas in S. H. Brooks, *Designs for Cottages and Villa Architecture*, London, (1840). One is shown in Chapter Two. Vincent J. Scully II, "Romantic Rationalism and the Expression of Structure in Wood: Downing, Wheeler, Gardner, and the 'Stick Style,' 1840–1876," *The Art Bulletin*, Vol. XXXV, no. 2, June 1953, pp. [121]–142.

20. Downing, *Country Houses*, p. 128.

21. A. J. Downing, *Rural Essays*, New York, 1857, p. 188.

22. Calvert Vaux, *Villas and Cottages*, New York, 1857, illustrated p. 116, described pp. 111–112.

23. Charles P. Dwyer, *The Economic Cottage Builder*, Buffalo, etc., 1855, p. [63].

24. Wayne Andrews, "American Gothic," *American Heritage*, Vol. XXII, no. 6, October 1971, pp. [40]–41.

25. Interview with Mrs. Emily Post, daughter of Bruce Price, 13 January 1956.

26. Antoinette J. Downing and Vincent J. Scully II, *The Architectural Heritage of Newport Rhode Island*, Cambridge, 1952, Plates 205, 215.

27. *Ibid.*, p. 154.

28. *Inquirer and Mirror*, Nantucket, 1 March 1873, p. 2; *ibid.*, 15 March 1873, p. 2.

29. *A Picture of ye Patchwork Village, 'Sconset by ye Sea*, 1885; *The Credible Chronicles of the Patchwork Village*, 1886; *'Sconset by the Sea*, ca. 1893; and *'Sconset in a Nutshell*, n. d.; also "'Sconset Then and Now—a Retrospective Glance at the Patchwork Village," *Inquirer and Mirror*, 20 August 1885; "The 'Sconset Railroad," originally in the *Boston Herald* and reprinted in the *Nantucket Journal*, 6 August 1891; also the series, "The Old Houses on 'Sconset Bank," *Nantucket Journal*, August–September 1889.

30. As by Hinkle, Guild and Co., 365 West First Street, Cincinnati, Ohio, whose product was called Kansas and Nebraska Portable Cottages, evidently meant to be taken West. *Kentucky Statesman*, Lexington, Ky., 16 March 1855, p. 3. Also, *P. N. Skillings and D. B. Flint's Illustrated Catalogue of Portable Sectional Buildings*, patented 19 November 1861, with offices in Boston and New York. A 12-by-16-foot lodge or railroad station cost $125, a 20-by-40-foot hospital $550. Two or three men could erect one in three hours.

III

EARLY BUNGALOWS ALONG
THE EASTERN SEABOARD

AS MIGHT BE EXPECTED, there was a time lag between the first appearance of a house labeled "bungalow" in England and the first one in the
United States. The earliest specimen illustrated in this country's initial
building journal, the *American Architect and Building News*, which was
launched at Boston in 1876, was at Monument Beach, on Buzzards Bay
at the base of Cape Cod. It was designed by William Gibbons Preston of
Boston in 1879. Like the Birchington bungalow it was a summer home
on the ocean; but it was picturesque, two storied, and of frame construction. Its framing was exposed, in the manner of Brooks's irregular
villas and Downing's Swiss cottage, which came to be known as the
Stick Style; but its roof lines were low and predominantly horizontal,
and gables had wide bargeboards. Walls were sheathed primarily in
clapboards, with a few upper areas in shingles. Windows had many-
paned upper sashes yet only one or two panes below, which was to
become a prevalent type of bungalow fenestration. Veranda posts were

Fig. 44

44. Bungalow at Monument Beach, Mass. W. G. Preston, Architect.
American Architect and Building News, 27 March 1880.

45. Remodeled House for Frank Hill Smith, Falmouth, Mass. Frank Hill Smith, Architect. *American Architect and Building News*, 23 October 1886.

rustic and had diagonal braces, in contrast to neatly shaped bracket supports above. The plan shows the center axis of the house shared by a stairhall and living room, the latter with fireplace and bay window (containing a window seat) for the view. In the upper-right corner of the plan is the dining room, with two windows in one outer wall and glazed double doors in the other; pantries and kitchen are below. Three rooms on the other side apparently serve as sleeping apartments. Wash rooms are provided. Additional chambers would be on the floor above. The layout, involving adjoining rectangular rooms, a minimum of corridors, recessed entrance shelter, projecting living room, and encompassing veranda, bears affinities to that of Kipling's British government *dāk*-bungalow in India, though probably by coincidence. Except for French doors and simple posts there is little else about the Monument Beach bungalow reminiscent of the East Indian prototype.

Fig. 2

A building that deserves consideration in a survey of American bungalows (though not claimed as such), because of some of its physical characteristics, still stands seven miles south of Monument Beach on Buzzards Bay. It is the historic house on Locust Street in Falmouth that architect Frank Hill Smith remodeled for his own use in 1881. The old central chimney and clapboard siding remained, and the conscientious use of small-paned sashes (rather than casements), turned posts, a bulging bay window, and paneled gables probably were thought of as Colonial Revival. The horizontality of hovering eaves of a roof that is none *Fig. 45* too steep and a balcony covered by imbricated shingles over which vines are hanging is inventive, making this a transitional bungalow design. The rustic fence is a bit of quaintness dating from the natural-landscape era; a picket fence now replaces it.

In the United States the term bungalow soon shifted to the year-round house. Arnold W. Brunner, a New York City architect, designed a long, low form, nominally ''Queen Anne'' in style, whose plainness was relieved by half-timbering on a gable and dormer window, and there were baluster posts and banistered railings in the end galleries. A perspective sketch of it appeared as the frontispiece in a book of *Cottages*, representing ''Medium and Low Cost Houses,'' compiled and edited by Brunner in 1884. The plan, appearing in Plate XVII, shows a poorly *Fig. 46* lighted hall substituting for the living room, with an adjoining (and larger) dining room, each with corner fireplace in a chimney that also serves the kitchen. Stairs in a back entry ascend to the garret, which may *Fig. 47* be used ''for dormitories,'' undoubtedly referring only to the near end,

46. Perspective Sketch of a Bungalow. A. W. Brunner,
Cottages or Hints on Economic Building, New York, 1884.

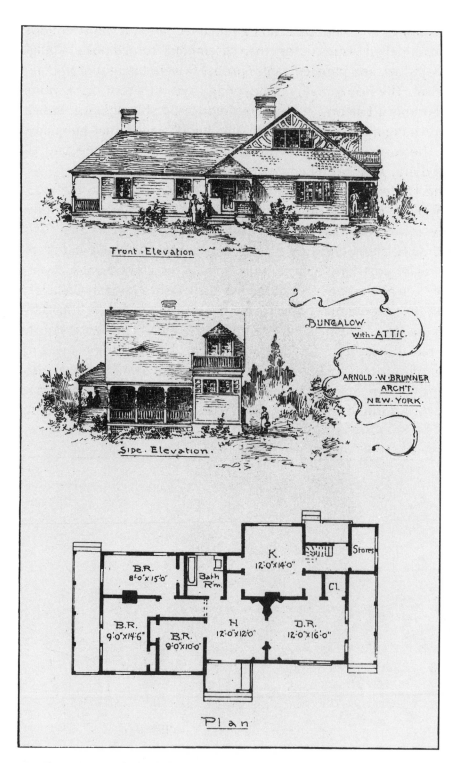

47. Elevations and Plan of the Frontispiece Bungalow.
Brunner, *Cottages or Hints on Economic Building*.

48. Bungalow at Paterson, N.J. Charles Edwards, Architect.
Building, 12 March 1887.

where the windows are concentrated. This house is a bungalow by
virtue of the main bedrooms being downstairs. Three of them are
connected to a bath by a side passage; or at least they were meant to
be, as Brunner comments that "the door of the bath-room and that of
the bed-room opposite are misplaced, and should open into the corridor," rather than to the hall.

Architect Charles Edwards of Paterson, New Jersey, seems to have
applied the word "bungalow" arbitrarily to a residence he designed in
his home town. Paterson, twelve miles inland from the northern tip of
Manhattan Island, is twenty miles from the ocean (if New York Bay may
be considered part of the Atlantic), and therefore, it is no resort area;
also the building is considerably larger and more substantial than its
bungalow predecessors. Except for the entrance pent, the stone walls
rise to between the second-story window sill and the second-floor ceiling levels. Porchless, its forms are compact, with polygonal projecting   *Fig. 48*
vestibule and bay window, a rounded corner "tower" at one end and a
dormer window at the other, and an "eyebrow" window piercing the
roof between them. The entry and dormer shapes, stubby chimneys,
and small-paned multilight windows resemble elements of the Brunner
bungalow just seen. They also relate to the heavy-handed Romanesque
Revival style used by Henry Hobson Richardson, Peabody and Stearns,

THE AMERICAN BUNGALOW

49. Perspective and Plan of Bungalow House for J. R. Pitcher at Grindstone Neck, Me. W. W. Kent, Architect. *Architecture and Building*, 25 March 1893.

E. M. Wheelwright, John Calvin Stevens, McKim, Mead and White and others during the early 1880s.[1] The arch in the front plane of the oriel window (as stated in Chapter One) is a motif proper to the "Queen Anne" style and substantiates the eclecticism of Edwards's house. Forms and materials anticipate some of R. A. Briggs's English bungalows of several years later.

Fig. 15

Surpassing the Edwards house in size and complexity, but more fragile structurally, was the "Bungalow House" for James R. Pitcher at Grindstone Neck, Maine, designed by W. W. Kent of New York City. "Bungalow" here refers to its seasonal aspect. The built-up platform recalls Romanesque Revival stonework, but walls of the building proper are stuccoed, clapboarded, or shingled, differing from the Stick Style in that no structural members show, surfaces being completely covered by a "skin." The Pitcher bungalow follows the form of shingled houses designed by Boston Architect William Ralph Emerson for sites at Mount Desert and Bar Harbor, Maine, dating from 1879 to 1885. Two contained polygonal and circular rooms and rounded terraces, and the third incorporated polygons with a wing jutting out at an obtuse angle.[2] The incorporation of these elements in the Grindstone Neck project is not without merit. The entrance from the land side leads to an irregular space of considerable openness, flowing right and left into the dining and living

Fig. 49

rooms, beyond into an apsidal-ended library, and with a screen of columns completing the near side of a circular reception room with a seat incorporated into the wide window opposite. There is a three-sided porch, and a concave terrace wall with stairs at either end leading down to the beach. Above, the long box dormer at the angle, necessitated by the dipping roof over the porch, seems an awkward addendum on what is properly a two-storied house. Windows in the gable indicate rooms in the garret. The Brunner design had a hall in place of a living room; the Kent house has a living room and also a more centrally located quasi-formal room (labeled "R. R."); but the single focal room in the Preston house (without designation) was to become the typical living room in the bungalow (Chapter Eight).

In 1896 the *American Architect and Building News* featured a page of beautifully delineated house sketches by Boston Architect Julius Adolph Schweinfurth, who, some years later, was to make the drawings of the Cuban farmhouse seen in Chapter Two.[3] His buildings were located at Brookline, Milton, and Newton Centre, Massachusetts. The houses in

Figs. 23, 24

50. Sketches of Five Houses in the Vicinity of Boston. J. A. Schweinfurth, Architect. *American Architect and Building News*, 22 August 1896.

THE AMERICAN BUNGALOW

Fig. 50

the two upper and lower left corners of the sheet are based on English manors, that in the lower right is American Colonial, and the specimen in the center is an original bungalow creation. It had been designed for the William H. Lincoln estate at Newton Centre in 1895. The treatment is strong and simple, with low-pitched conic and hipped roofs whose overhangs cast deep shadows on shingled walls, and out of which rise substantial chimney shafts, heavily capped. A parapeted terrace swings around the curved pavilion at the left. No plan is given, but it is obvious from the bank of windows that this is the living room. One can grasp the clarity and power of this feature by comparing it to the same relationship of round room (virtually concealed) and surrounding terraces at the Pitcher bungalow-house. Projecting bay windows, snug under the eaves, on the near side, denote bedrooms. The kitchen ell can be seen extending from the far side of the house at the right. The continuation of the terrace wall out equal to the roof overhang makes a covered back porch, calling attention to the fact that these surrounding shelters are virtually galleries without upright supports (Frontispiece). Although differently handled, they are equivalent to the feature on early Flemish

Fig. 18

houses on Long Island. The round and polygonal forms recall the tower accent on Haskell's Eyrie, built forty years earlier and shown in vignette

Fig. 36

on the Llewellyn Park map. The respective building masses tie in with their settings, Haskell's with the vertical prominence of Eagle Rock, and Lincoln's with the gently undulating meadows west of Boston. The keying

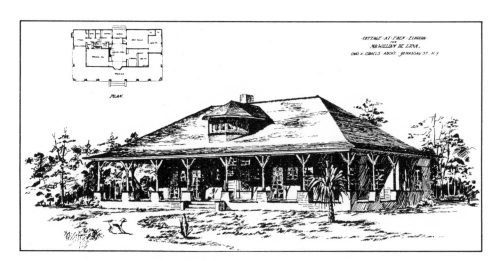

51. William de Luna Cottage at Eden, Fla. Charles H. Israels, Architect. *Architecture and Building*, 29 April 1893.

in of the bungalow with its environment in the Schweinfurth drawing is not unlike sketches in the Downing books at mid century, indicating that the Hudson River aesthete paved the way for the trend that bungalow landscaping was to take in the United States.

Figs. 29, 30, 31

The Schweinfurth Colonial Revival house represents a late-nineteenth-century American movement that manifested itself in the bungalow in the form of borrowings from the Lower Mississippi Valley raised-cottage type with a peristyle porch, reflected in the Louisiana Pavilion at the World's Columbian Exposition. However, early bungalow versions sat low to the ground, like the cottage designed by John Hall, and as in the William de Luna cottage at Eden, Florida. The architect was Charles H. Israels of New York City. It and the Hall house are of about equal size, both as regards enclosed volume and open galleries. The Florida version has thin bracketed posts on pedestals, rather than columns, no railings, a single chimney, but a polygonal dormer window on the long plane of the roof. A living room replaces the passage bisecting the plan. A dining room balances a library and bedroom to either side at the front, and the rest of the space is divided arbitrarily. A stairway adjoining the kitchen corridor suggests sleeping accommodations above. Although employing the nineteenth-century term for a vacation house, "cottage," it is significant that Israels modified the design into a bungalow for an article that was published in the April, 1909, issue of *Good Housekeeping*. Called "The Busy Man's Bungalow," Israels points out that the middle-income New Yorker could afford a house out of the noise and confusion of the city, yet within commuting distance, if located north of Long Island Sound, in the Connecticut hills. Land, builders' fees, materials, and their transportation would amount to little more than one-third what they would cost in Greater New York City. Setting aside $1,000 for the site, the bungalow as presented would come to a total of $4,000. It has a large (15-by-28-foot) living room, four bedrooms, kitchen, bathroom, six closets, and a refrigerator recess. For economy's sake, passages are minimal, and walls and ceilings are of planks instead of plaster. The living room rises to the rafters, which, with the underside of the shingles, are "stained without varnish." Floored sleeping spaces are in the garret over the bedrooms, reached by ladders in the back corners of the living room, for extra guests. Lack of insulation and the great open upper space would be a drain on heat coming from the one fireplace in the house, but it was meant to be occupied only during summers. The round Tuscan columns to the front veranda give this

Fig. 21

Figs. 25, 51

Fig. 52

Fig. 53

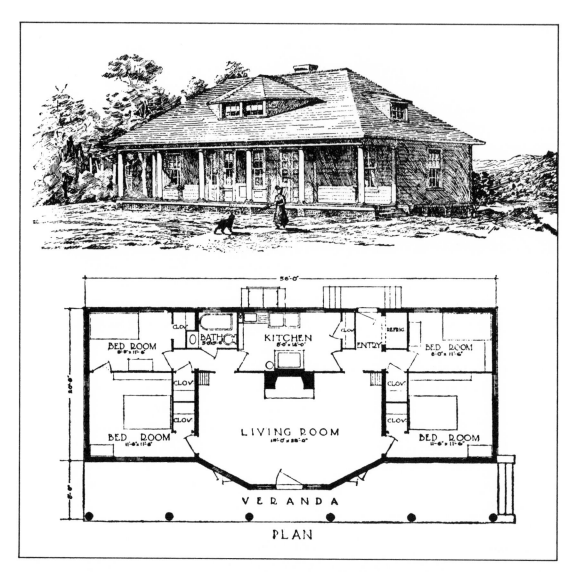

52, 53. "The Busy Man's Bungalow." Perspective Sketch and Floor Plan.
Charles H. Israels, Architect. *Good Housekeeping*, April 1909.

"bungalow" a more traditional look than the posted "cottage" in Florida,
furnishing a substantial argument for reversing their designations.

Bungalow is certainly a suitable term for the vacation house that
New York architect W. Gedney Beatty built on Lake Onawa (about 20
Fig. 54 miles south of Greenville), Maine, about 1898. It is nearly square, its
only significant dormer merges with the chimney stack, and the posts
and railings of its encircling porch are rustic, like the supports at Monu-

ment Beach. No floor plan is given, but with a bay window centered on the front and symmetrically placed openings right and left its arrangement must have been similar to those by Charles H. Israels. However, the position of the chimney either denotes a living-room fireplace at the side of the house or else serves a kitchen.

These low-lying houses in Maine, Florida, and presumably Connecticut resemble a portable structure manufactured by the Ducker Company of New York City, which, at the turn of the century, supplied "Bungalows, cottages, homes, garages, hospitals, school houses and churches."[4] An example of the first kind had been assembled for Walter Winans of Surrenden Park, England, in the mid 1880s. It was reported, twenty-five years later, as being in "as good condition today as when first erected." This long rectangular construction bears affinities to the first native British bungalow, which also was "portable." This import from America would have adopted the bungalow title easily in the British Isles.

Fig. 55
Fig. 13

One of the largest bungalows of the peristyle variety on the East Coast was at Robbins Point on Grindstone Island, New York. It was designed by David Knickerbocker Boyd of Philadelphia. It also was for

54. Bungalow near Onawa, Me. W. Gedney Beatty, Architect.
American Architect and Building News, 26 November 1898.

Order today, shipped tomorrow, erected the next day and you live in it the following day, because we have millions of feet of sections in our mills ready for erecting any size, style or shape of structure anywhere.

Bungalows, cottages, homes, garages, hospitals, school houses and churches or any building that can be made of wood. While our structures are portable they are also permanent.

Tell us the size of the building you have in mind, we will send you a sketch free and quote you price. Send today for our book of houses, free.

We made this structure 25 years ago for Mr. Walter Winans, of Surrenden Park, England, who states it is in as good condition today as when first erected.

In the past quarter of a century we have made thousands of such buildings for customers all over the world. Let us make one for you.

DUCKER COMPANY *Manufacturers of* SECTIONAL-PORTABLE-READY-MADE STRUCTURES.
277 BROADWAY, NEW YORK

55. Portable Bungalow Manufactured by the Ducker Company of New York City, Erected in England during the mid 1880s. *Country Life in America*, 15 May 1911.

56. Bungalow at Robbins Point, Grindstone Island, N.Y. D. K. Boyd, Architect. *The Craftsman*, August 1907.

57. "An East Indian Bungalow at Prospect Park South,"
The Brooklyn Daily Eagle, 7 June 1902.

seasonal occupancy, and it stood on a rocky slope at the water's edge, raised on great piers. The heavy masonry supports below, lighter wood posts above, and the roof reaching out to narrow cornices (rather than to a full entablature) recall those of the Louisiana State exhibit at the World's Columbian Exposition. All rooms of the Grindstone Island bungalow are on the principal floor, the lower and upper zones serving only for storage. Walls are covered by shingles stained only by the weather, and railings and uprights carrying the roof are natural trunks and branches of trees, as in the Lake Onawa example.

Fig. 56

A bizarre intruder into the bungalow realm at the beginning of this century was the "East Indian Bungalow at Prospect Park South," whose intended image appeared in the *Brooklyn Daily Eagle* during the summer of 1903. It was to be erected by New York entrepreneur Dean Alvord, and was to follow the form of its attested prototype "as closely as the climatic conditions will allow." The builder is said to have collected special materials "for a house of this character," and the interior finish and grounds were to be laid out in perfect harmony. Its exotic features were intended to make it "a good seller." The building was finished within the year, and its picture accompanied a for-sale adver-

Fig. 57

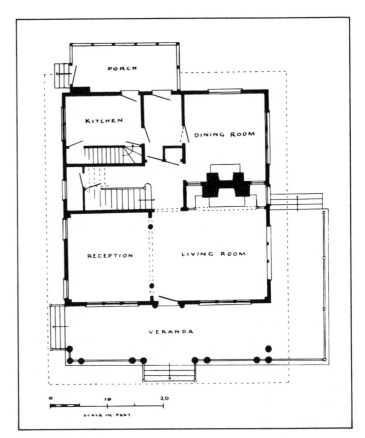

58, 59. Japanese House and Garden at Prospect Park South, Brooklyn, N.Y. J. J. Petit and J. C. Green, Architects. *Country Life in America*, July 1903. First-floor plan measured and drawn by the author.

tisement in the July issue of *Country Life in America*. The building had *Fig. 58*
become larger, the second story advanced over the veranda, and the
roof was pushed up, exposing a full front gable. The style claim had
been corrected from Indian to Japanese. Embellishments were heavy
and considerably more elaborate than on the Canmack cottage at Tuxedo Park, being in the Tokugawa palace–temple manner. The architects *Fig. 37*
were identified as John J. Petit and James C. Green, with the "garden by
Mr. Chogoro Sugai, the color scheme and decoration by Mr. Shunsi
Ishikawa, all under the direction of the Japanese contractor, Mr. Saburo
Arai."[5] This explains why details were more authentic than the general
conception. The plan was compact but open, with grilles flanking
chimneybreasts between dining and living rooms, and seats in the inglenook of the latter. The house contained six bedrooms, and its bathing *Fig. 59*
facilities included a "porcelain Roman bathtub, also needle and shower
baths." It was priced to sell for $26,500. The landscaping has disappeared,
but the house still stands at 131 Buckingham Road, Brooklyn.

During the summer following the completion of the Alvord house,
the amusement park called Dreamland opened in Coney Island, at the
far end of Brooklyn. Among its fanciful buildings was a Japanese-style
pavilion dominated by a pagoda superstructure.[6] A sign over its portal
testified to its exhibit as being the "AIRSHIP," obviously derived from the
Orville and Wilbur Wright achievement at Kitty Hawk in December of
1903. Inasmuch as John J. Petit is known to have designed some of the
buildings at Dreamland, one assumes that the Airship Building was his,
too.

The form of the Airship Building surfaced domestically as a vacation
retreat built at Jamaica, Long Island, a few years later. It was illustrated
on the front cover of the January 1910, issue of *Bungalow Magazine*, a
monthly not yet a year old. An accompanying article identified it as "A *Fig. 60*
JAPANESE TORRI," built "for Miss Blanche Sloan, the actress, whose artistic temperament required a summer house that not only provides all of
the requirements of occidental life, but also embodies much of the
refinement that is invariably present in the architecture of the land of
the Mikado."[7] Jamaica at that time was an actors' summer colony. Miss
Sloan was known as the Queen of the Air, which is not to say that she
was an aviatrix but an aerialist. Her vacation hermitage was not a "TORRI"
(*torii*—Japanese for a ceremonial gateway) but a pagoda-inspired bungalow. It contained a living room, kitchen, bedroom, and bath on the first
floor, a second-story living room as well, and an open third level where

60. Blanche Sloan Bungalow at Jamaica, Long Island, N.Y., as Depicted on the Front Cover of *Bungalow Magazine*, January 1910.

THE JANUARY 1910
BUNGALOW MAGAZINE
10¢ PER COPY
VOL I. NO. 11

HENRY L. WILSON • PUBLISHER
COPP BLDG •   GREAT NORTHERN BLDG
LOS ANGELES CAL •   CHICAGO ILL

61. First- and Second-floor Plans of the Blanche Sloan Bungalow. *Bungalow Magazine*, January 1910.

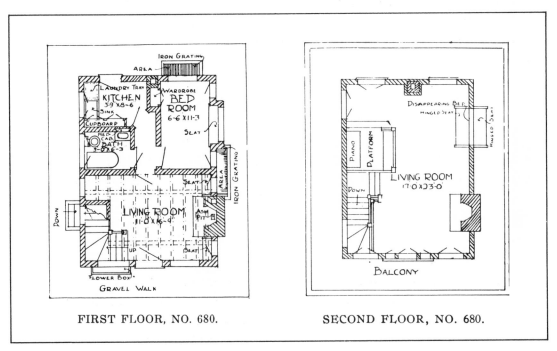

FIRST FLOOR, NO. 680.   SECOND FLOOR, NO. 680.

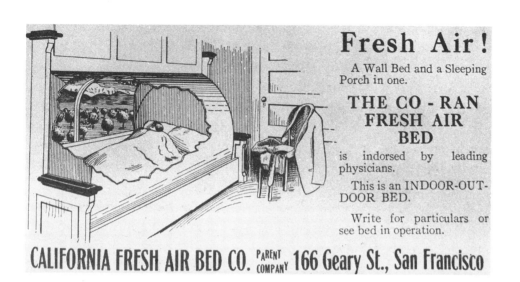

62. Indoor-outdoor Bed with Roll Top, Manufactured by the California Fresh Air Bed Company, San Francisco. *Architect and Engineering*, March 1914.

63. Blanche Sloan Bungalow, Jamaica, Long Island, N.Y. Photo 1954.

Fig. 61

Fig. 62

Fig. 63

she practiced on the trapeze. The upper living room featured a platformed piano and a disappearing bed, the latter half projecting onto the balcony for outdoor sleeping, a space-conserving version of the sleeping porch. An athlete like Miss Sloan would have appreciated the healthful advantages of being in the fresh air. The arched bridge and stone lantern shown in the magazine cover illustration were as illusory as the term used for the house. A photograph of 1913 includes the concrete-block wall and gateposts capped by putti that still exist. The balcony has been screened in and the top story enclosed.

The "torri" is reminiscent of a house that was built on Biscayne Bay, Miami, Florida, in 1905. Resembling Miss Sloan's, it appropriately was referred to as the "Bungoda."[8]

The first quarter-century of bungalow building in the United States produced specimens that fall into six categories. They are the Stick Style, the Shingle Style, the quasi-Romanesque or Rock Style, the peristyle house, and the Japanese style, all of which were derived from architectural statements previously made in America. Also there was one exceptionally fine original composition, which both stood for and anticipated others of the bungalow movement's top achievements. Undoubtedly quantities of examples similar to these were called bungalows in popular parlance, but they failed to become perpetuated as such in print for our information.

NOTES

1. Such as the Ames Gate Lodge, Easton; "Kragsyde," Manchester-by-the Sea, Mass.; E. C. Stedman house, Newcastle Island, Portsmouth Harbor, James Hopkins Smith house, Falmouth Foreside, near Portland, Me.; and the Casino at Narragansett Pier, R.I. Vincent J. Scully II, *The Shingle Style*, New Haven and London, 1955, illustrations 55–56, 61–63, 77–78, 87–88, and 117–118.

2. *Ibid.*, illustrations 46, 82, and 83.

3. J. A. Schweinfurth was associated with the firm of Peabody and Stearns, Boston, at this time, having returned to the East Coast from Cleveland. He resided at Brookline from 1869 to 1922 and built his bungalow home at 11 Boulder Road, Chestnut Hill. (Interview with J. A. Schweinfurth II, 2 September 1954).

4. *Country Life in America*, 15 May 1911, p. 58.

5. *Ibid.*, July 1903, p. 169.

6. Illustrated in Clay Lancaster, *Japanese Influence in America*, New York, 1963 and 1983, p. 130.

7. *Bungalow Magazine*, January 1910, p. 321.

8. John Gifford, "A Bungoda," *The House Beautiful*, November 1905, p. 49.

IV

THE PLACE OF THE PRAIRIE HOUSE IN THE BUNGALOW MOVEMENT

EARLY EXAMPLES along the East Coast did not leave a single impression of what the bungalow was or what it was going to be. It represented only the beginning of the phenomenon, and the bungalow had not yet attained a definitive form. Its label was applied by persons with but an imperfect idea as to its precise meaning. The early period represented a groping; it contributed to but did not attain a culmination. As we move from the Atlantic seaboard to the Great Lakes region we also come to a later era. The creative phase there followed an international show held at Chicago, the World's Columbian Exposition of 1893, seventeen years after the Philadelphia Centennial, and, as in the East, there was a few years' delay before the impact of what the fair offered was realized in local building. It might be mentioned that during the second quarter of the nineteenth century, while Hudson Valley aesthetes were creating romantic architectural modes, practical Chicago devised and made widespread use of the balloon frame.[1] It consisted of a wall skeleton made up of uniformly spaced uprights (of 2 x 4s, 2 x 6s, or 2 x 8s) connecting sill and plate; this system was to be used almost universally in bungalow construction. A regional self-sufficiency crystallized at the end of the nineteenth century in the emergence of a Chicago school of architecture, which was to generate a distinct domestic type called the "prairie house." The prairie house matured at the base of Lake Michigan at about the same time the bungalow took on definitive form farther west. Being contemporaries, the two latched onto a number of traits in common, and it will be our business here to concentrate on the Midwestern manifestation.

A persisting characteristic of the Chicago school is its ingrown development, meaning that it has centered around its own works, resisting outside influences other than those that chanced to come to its own doorstep. The modern phase got off to a start coeval with the appearance of the first bungalow in the construction of the seven-storied Leiter Building, of 1879. It was designed by William Le Baron Jenney, who had acquired sound technical training in Paris, and was to implant a number of other ornaments in that seedbed of high-rise archi-

THE AMERICAN BUNGALOW

64. South Pavilion of the Japanese Hōōden at the World's Columbian Exposition, Chicago. *Inland Architect and News Record*, October 1893.

tecture in The Loop. The Chicago School became aware of its identity with the establishment of its mouthpiece, *The Inland Architect and News Record*, in 1883. Within the next few years, two downtown colossuses were built, Henry Hobson Richardson's Marshall Field Wholesale Store, 1885, and Dankmar Adler and Louis Sullivan's Auditorium Building, 1887–89.[2] Richardson had been a successful architect of impressive public buildings in the Romanesque Revival style before his work in Chicago, and he shattered a local tradition by raising a design in his fully developed manner in this provincial community.

The second purlieu of the Chicago School, and that which concerns us here, was domestic and in the suburbs. Compared to the great towering hulks in The Loop its structures were miniscule. Also, its crystallization began after the downtown counterpart had attained its apex just cited, which was after the Columbian Exposition. The staid Neoclassic motif of the fair, devised by the New York group of architects and decried locally, was of no more use to the residential than to the downtown theatre of operations; but the fair presented a contrary import, that exerted considerable influence upon the upcoming trend. This was the Japanese Hōōden on Wooded Island. It was a more formidable exhibit than what the Japanese had erected at the Philadelphia Centennial and was composed of three connected pavilions, showing various period styles inside but unified externally by exposed structural timbers enframing rectangles of plaster, accentuated horizontals of platform and eaves, and graceful roofs. If most observers failed to note its flexibility of outer walls and plan (more than three-fourths of the exterior and all interior panels were movable), few could miss the exquisite craftsmanship, good proportions and clean-cut forms, and color and texture contrasts in the natural materials utilized.

Fig. 64

Chicago dwellings showed no remarkable qualities before the Exposition. If we take as an example Louis Sullivan's summer home on Biloxi Bay, Mississippi, we are back to the peristyle bungalow. Other contemporaries confirm this as a Chicago type.[3] Said to have been designed by Frank Lloyd Wright in 1890, while employed in Sullivan's office, early photographs show a somewhat different building.[4] The one here illus-

Fig. 65

65. Louis Sullivan's Vacation House at Ocean Springs, Miss. *Architectural Record*, June 1905.

trated may be a replacement, though dating no later than the first few years of this century. Roof, walls, and piers are shingled. A veranda spans the front of five rooms in a row, including a living room in the center, expanding into a dining room, and three bedrooms, the outer two projecting as polygons. An ell on axis behind the living room contained kitchen, pantries, a bathroom and servants' quarters. A flower garden figured prominently in front of the house, and a complete rural establishment was on the grounds (Chapter Nine).[5]

Fig. 66

One of the first Chicago School houses to strike a new chord was Frank Lloyd Wright's Chauncey L. Williams residence, built in 1895 at River Forest. As pointed out by the foremost of Wright's publicists, the steep roof and artfully incorporated boulders seem to have been suggested by Japanese woodblock prints, which Wright collected.[6] But in addition the design stresses horizontal lines and zones of stuccoed surface, which would have come from the Hōōden.

Fig. 67

Two years later architect George Maher conceived the John Farson house in Wright's hometown of Oak Park. The wide, three-bayed bulk bears affinities to Frank Lloyd Wright's first independent commission

66. Chauncey L. Williams House, River Forest, Ill. Frank Lloyd Wright, Architect. Photo Courtesy the Art Institute of Chicago.

67. John Farson House, Oak Park, Ill. George Maher, Architect.
The Inland Architect, November 1899.

after leaving Sullivan's office in 1893, the W. H. Winslow house in River Forest.[7] The Winslow house, however, is divided horizontally by two materials, brick below and terra cotta in repeated relief patterns, slightly overhanging, above. There is no front porch, though an arch to the porte-cochere shows around the corner on the right flank. Also, in Wright's design the roof is unencumbered by ridge motif, dormer, or parapet, and eaves are exceedingly deep. The Maher scheme establishes the monumentality of parapets, terraces, and steps, sweeping left and right, keying in these elements with the terrain, and thus expanding the architectural composition, with its cubic-volume consciousness of plastered walls, and the role of void shadows as a decorative element.

The prairie house hit its stride in 1900 in two adjoining residences designed by Frank Lloyd Wright and built at the south end of Harrison Avenue on the river in Kankakee, Illinois. The larger was for B. Harley Bradley, and the smaller for his brother-in-law, Warren Hickox. Con- *Figs. 68, 69* spicuous are hovering roofs, eaves considerably extended, thrust forward at the apex (as in Japanese Shintō shrines), and the soffits of the eaves slanting upward to reduce bargeboards to the thinnest possible edge. Stuccoed walls also are lightened by showing nowhere more than a few feet tall and—at least in the Hickox house—are divided vertically

68. B. Harley Bradley House, Kankakee, Ill.
Frank Lloyd Wright, Architect. Photo 1954.

by half-timbering, as in the Hōōden. The sinking of the building into the ground, asymmetrical expansion of low forms, wide setting of the roofs, and group treatment of the fenestration hark back almost a century to Joseph Gandy's four attached cottages. The first-floor plan of the *Fig. 8* small Warren Hickox house shows a remarkable flow of space, in the way the reception hall leads to the living room, which in turn opens at either end into the polygonal music and dining rooms, and there are *Fig. 70* glass doors onto the terrace. It was the application of what Louis Sullivan had trained Wright to think of as "organic architecture"—of a building design developing from the inside out.

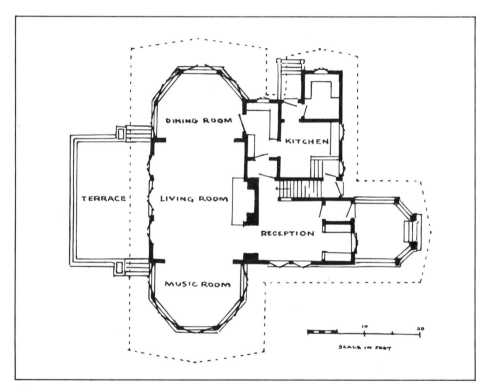

69, 70. Warren Hickox House, Kankakee, Ill. Frank Lloyd Wright, Architect. Photo by Henry Fuermann. *Architectural Record*, July 1905. First-floor plan drawn by the author.

There is a remarkable similarity between the work of English architect Joseph Gandy and that of Frank Lloyd Wright, which may be seen readily by juxtaposing the former's attached cottages alongside one of the Chicago master's prairie houses covered by a hipped roof. The

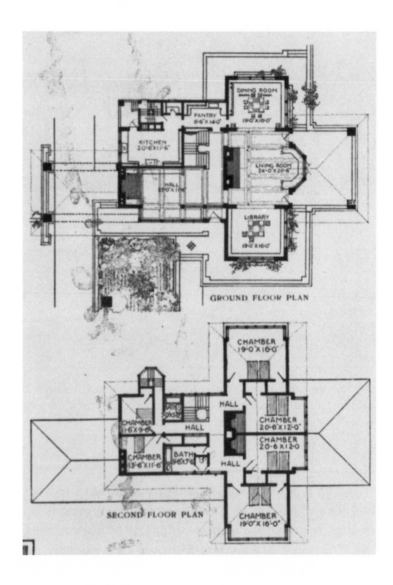

71. Perspective, Floor Plans, and Section *(opposite)* of a Project for the Curtis Publishing Company: A House in a Prairie Town. Frank Lloyd Wright, Architect. *Ladies' Home Journal*, February 1901.

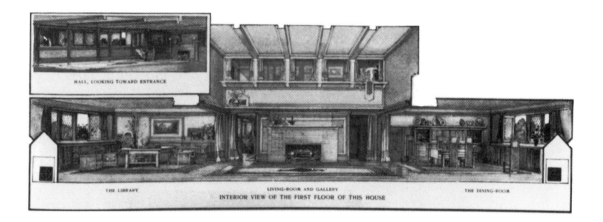

HALL, LOOKING TOWARD ENTRANCE

THE LIBRARY   LIVING-ROOM AND GALLERY   THE DINING-ROOM
INTERIOR VIEW OF THE FIRST FLOOR OF THIS HOUSE

archetype was designed for the *Ladies Home Journal* and published in their February, 1901, issue. The main differences between the Gandy and Wright buildings are that the latter divides the already horizontal forms further by plinths or footings and window sills carried across the masonry. Fenestration therefore is more contained. Constructed examples consist of the Ward W. Willitts house (1902) at Highland Park, and the smaller Isabel Roberts house (1908) at River Forest.[8] In the latter year Wright built the E. A. Gilmore house elevated on a terrace at Madison, Wisconsin.[9] One looks up at its pointed-balcony "nose," receding "body," and outstretched "wings" that led to its having been nicknamed the Airplane House. Nevertheless it is as stationary and enduring an example of the prairie house as has ever been conceived.

Figs. 8, 71

The example from the Chicago School that literally as well as theoretically justifies the inclusion of prairie houses in this exposition on bungalows is the Bungalow on the Point. It was conceived by the firm of Purcell, Feick and Elmslie, with branch offices in Minneapolis and Chicago, for Charles R. Crane in 1911–12.[10] Crane, a manufacturer of plumbing equipment in the Windy City, had a summer home on Juniper Point at Woods Hole on lower Cape Cod, for which he had engaged Purcell, Feick and Elmslie to design a gardener's cottage in 1910. The commission a year or two later concerned a vacation house for Crane's daughter and son-in-law, Dr. and Mrs. Harold C. Bradley.[11] It was to be located far out on the promontory, with magnificent water views in three directions. The architects devised a narrow, two-storied, crosswise form, with a lower rounded projection in front surrounded by windows, and another long ell at the back. Resembling the correspond-

Fig. 72

THE AMERICAN BUNGALOW

Frontis.

Fig. 73
Fig. 74

ing member in Schweinfurth's bungalow on the Lincoln estate fifteen years earlier, the projecting pavilion was the living room, with exposed beam ceiling, a great arched fireplace at the back, and a continuous seat built beneath the ring of windows. The "rooms" to either side of the center chimney were originally open porches. The plan was "airplane," with services at the back. The upstairs contained four bedrooms, two-and-a-half baths, and two sleeping porches. Planting was to occupy the ledges at either end, as well as in the ground beyond the lower terraces. The Bungalow on the Point, while holding to the prairie-house shape,

72. The Bungalow on the Point, Woods Hole, Mass. Purcell, Feick and Elmslie, Architects, Photo 1954.

73. Living Room Detail in the Bungalow on the Point. Photo 1954.

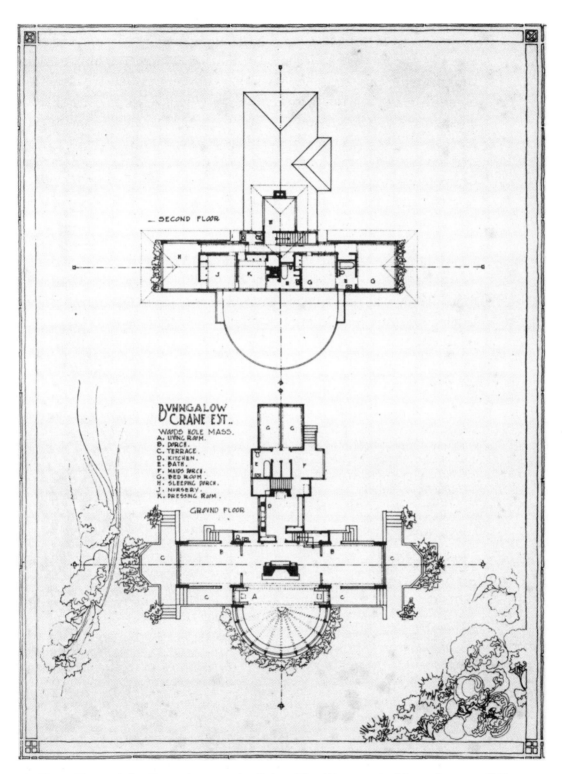

74. Floor Plans of the Bungalow on the Point. *The Western Architect*, January 1913.

departs from it in having shingled walls. Probably this was a concession to traditional architecture here in its New England setting. The same might be said for the heavy central chimney, bold upper-story overhangs, and the small, leaded casement windows upstairs. Even with these indigenous features, a storm of local protest greeted what was considered its incongruous appearance on the cape, causing Charles R. Crane to make a hurried trip to "see what all the hullabaloo was about." He wired back that the building in its site looked "wonderful."[12] One wonders if the name "Bungalow on the Point" were coined by the architects as a way of acclimating the essentially prairie-house design with an established East Coast nomenclature?

Purcell, Feick and Elmslie followed up this project with a remarkably similar house for Edward W. Decker, sited on a wooded knoll overlooking Lake Minnetonka in Minnesota. Its walls were of brick, not shingles, the chimney was moved back from the roof ridge, and drawings were labeled "house" or "Country dwelling," not "bungalow."[13]

NOTES

1. St. Mary's Church (1833), Chicago, is thought to be the first building of balloon-frame construction. The system was popularized in William E. Bell's *Carpentry Made Easy . . . with Specific Instructions for Building Balloon Frames . . .* , Philadelphia, 1858, and later advocated in George E. Woodward's *Woodward's Country Houses*, New York, 1865.

2. Sigfried Giedion, *Space, Time and Architecture*, Cambridge, 1948, pp. 291–315; M. G. Van Rensselaer, *Henry Hobson Richardson and His Works*, New York, 1888, pp. 95–97; Hugh Morrison, *Louis Sullivan*, New York, ca. 1935, pp. 80–110.

3. Such as the W. C. Egan house, Egandale, on Lake Michigan. *Country Life in America*, July 1902, p. lxv.

4. Henry-Russell Hitchcock, *In the Nature of Materials*, New York, 1942, p. 11, figure 4 (facing p. 14).

5. Lyndon P. Smith, "The Home of an Artist–Architect," *Architectural Record*, June 1905, pp. [471]–490.

6. Hitchcock, *In the Nature of Materials*, p. 26.

7. *Ibid.*, figure 25.

8. *Ibid.*, figures 73, 154.

9. *Ibid.*, figure 157.

10. William Gray Purcell, a graduate of Cornell University, who had apprenticed to Sullivan, established an architectural practice with George Feick at Minneapolis in 1906, and three years later they were joined by George Grant Elmslie (also Sullivan trained), after which they opened a second office in Chicago.

11. The Bradley house at Madison, Wis., had been designed several years earlier by Louis Sullivan's office, and Elmslie had worked on it.

12. Letter from William Gray Purcell to Dorothy Norman, 24 June 1949.

13. *The Western Architect*, special issues on Purcell, Feick and Elmslie, January 1913 (plan) and July 1915 (photographs both outside and inside).

V

THE BUNGALOW ON
ITS HOME GROUND
IN CALIFORNIA

WHEN CALIFORNIA was admitted to the Union as a state in 1850 its building stock consisted of scattered old Spanish missions, *rancho* and *hacienda* (farm) houses, a few American settlers' dwellings, and recently erected shacks in mining camps. The gold rush was then at a fever pitch. Within a quarter of a century the new-found wealth was to make San Francisco one of the great cities in the United States. The fabulous Palace Hotel was opened in 1875, its seven-tiered, arched and columned Grand Court sheltered under a glass roof. This architectural opulence at the hub was to be flung out to the suburbs by centrifugal force. Linden Towers, the Baroque-manner palace of James C. Flood, the "bonanza king," was completed in Menlo Park in 1879. One journalist called it "the most superb on our continent . . . no royal or ducal house in Europe excels it."[1] Perhaps Bruce Price was biased by such competition when he designed a country house to be built near San Francisco in 1886. It was in the Japanese-castle style, only the stone treatment normally reserved for the podium was carried over into first-story walls. As in his Canmack cottage in Tuxedo Park, crested plaques adorned upper panels, and roofs were flaring, with chimneys even more awkwardly emerging than in the Canmack cottage.

Fig. 75

By the early 1890s California's architectural exuberance had begun to simmer down to something more regional in character. The residence of S. Taylor, designed by architects Percy and Hamilton of San Francisco, and built at Winters about 1892, was a two-storied stuccoed cube showing Spanish influence. Bay windows, corner towers (one with arches), and the main eaves were bracketed, and the house embraced a center courtyard, into which the principal rooms and both stairways opened. Outdoor living had become recognized as an indigenous amenity.

Fig. 76

Prophetic of the trend domestic architecture was to take in California was the first West Coast bungalow pictured in the *American Architect*. Planned by A. Page Brown of San Francisco and built for J. D. Grant at Burlingame during the early 1890s, it was of the peristyle variety, only lifted high on masonry foundations because of the hillside site. Galler-

Fig. 77

75. Front Elevation for A House near San Francisco, Calif. Bruce Price, Architect. *Building*, 19 March 1887.

76. Perspective and Floor Plans of a House for S. Taylor, near Winters, Calif. Percy and Hamilton, Architects. *American Architect and Building News*, 7 January 1893.

ies were cantilevered and braced by struts, some portions being enclosed. The roof is picturesque, and the effect is partly that of the East
Indian prototype, partly Alpine, and partly American Swiss.

San Francisco asserted its importance and linked itself to Chicago by
hosting the California Midwinter International Exposition that opened
in January of 1894, attracting as many exhibits and star performances
(such as the Ferris wheel and John Philip Sousa's band) as it could from
the closing World's Columbian Exposition. Its architectural motif was
not Classic but Saracenic, with pointed or horseshoe-shaped arches,
saucer or bulbous domes on axial or end pavilions, and tall flanking
minarets or corner turrets. A. Page Brown designed the Manufacturers
and Liberal Arts Building. The fair was backed by San Francisco business-
men, including George Turner Marsh, a native Australian, who had
come to California and inaugurated America's first shop devoted exclusively to Japanese art in the Palace Hotel in 1876. Marsh had sojourned
in Nippon, and he conceived and sponsored a Japanese garden on an
acre of the exposition lot. Native workmen were employed to lay out
paths, streams, and pools, put in planting, and build bridges and an
assortment of structures, including a bazaar, two-storied gateway (*romon*),

*Fig. 2,
11, 31*

77. Bungalow for J. D. Grant, Burlingame, Calif. A. Page Brown, Architect.
American Architect and Building News, 8 June 1895.

78. View of the Japanese Tea Garden, San Francisco. A. Wittemann, *The California Midwinter International Exposition in Photogravure*, New York, 1894.

Fig. 78   small theatre, two-storied dwelling (*zashiki*), and several open shelters. The theatre and bazaar were removed after the fair, but most of the balance of the precinct survives as the enlarged Japanese Tea Garden in Golden Gate Park, the oldest of its kind in the United States. As at the Columbian Exposition, the Japanese display at the San Francisco Midwinter fair exerted more influence upon later regional home-building than all of the monumental theme halls combined.

Because of its mild climate and the reasonable availability of land, California became the destination of a new "gold" rush at the turn of the century. Young people came to make a living growing things, and older folk sought it as a retirement place, especially in the southern part of the state. Residents along the Pacific seaboard did not have the strong antique consciousness of those in the East, and with the casual living indulged in by the recently arrived, these factors were reflected in construction that developed. It was an ideal atmosphere for the bungalow, and an article by M. H. Lazear published in *The House Beautiful* in 1914 defined "The Evolution of the Bungalow." It said, in part:

> In the beginning was the barn. Persons of small means
> when they first came to California often found it desirable

to put all their money into land and the young orchards which were to make their fortunes. They decided to live themselves in a small structure which should be the barn of the future house. These barns were at first constructed with Eastern solidarity, with heavy posts and beams, and completely furnished on the inside as barns, with stalls, mangers and other like fittings. The human tenant generally decorated the carriage house with burlap or "Old Government Java" coffee bags, held in place by split bamboo strips; and this with a rough fireplace, a few good pieces of furniture, and the shadows of the rafters overhead, made a really delightful living-room. The great barn doors were generally left open, giving an outdoor effect very grateful to the lovers of the sun and space.

The next step was to build only the outside shell of a barn, dividing it into rooms with temporary partitions. . . .

Later, travelers from distant lands noticed the resemblance between these wide-spread, one-story houses and the East Indian "bungalow," and thenceforward these dwellings ceased to be temporary; but putting on wide verandas and a dignified name, sprang up in every direction as intentional homes. . . .

Eventually some great man discovered that as there was no snow and really no violent storms in California, a house could be made to stand up without a frame, that it could be built of nothing but upright boards reaching from sill to plate, with scantling as cross ties. . . . As lumber is very expensive here, having for the most part to be brought from Oregon, this economy of material gave an immense impetus to the building of small homes. . . . Most of the best bungalows are made of broad redwood boards with weather stripping, and are mill finished inside.[2]

The author goes on to say that the wood is left natural, though treated in a variety of ways. One of the cheapest is to dissolve asphalt in hot turpentine and apply it as a stain. A lump of asphalt, six inches square, could treat and preserve the surface of an entire house.

The "great man" credited with originating the bungalow of upright boards was not a single individual but a team of two brothers, Charles

Sumner Greene and Henry Mather Greene. They were educated for their profession first at the Manual Training High School in Saint Louis, and then at the Massachusetts Institute of Technology, from which they were graduated in 1891. After working for Boston architects, they went to California to visit their parents, and stayed to open an office at Pasadena in 1894. The young architects first designed in the popular styles of the day—including "Queen Anne," Old English, Spanish Mission, American Colonial, and Craftsman[3]—then in 1903 they hit upon a simple type using vertical boards, and an indigenous material that was to figure prominently in the bungalow movement, rounded boulders or cobblestones. Their first commission in this idiom has become a classic. This was the house for Arturo Bandini, in Pasadena, who speci-

Fig. 79   fied that its form should reflect the patio plan of his forebears' *ranchos* here. Slender posts and exposed rafters of the gallery encircling the

Fig. 22   courtyard are indeed like the Spanish immigrants' houses, but this lightness extended throughout, planks replacing thick adobe walls. A latticed pergola partly screened the open end of the quadrangle. The main rooms were located at the base of the U-form, with a bath and storage

Fig. 80   room near the junction in one arm, and bedrooms elsewhere. Circulation to all parts of the house, if not through connecting rooms, was by way of the open galleries. As no room of the bungalow was more than fifteen feet wide, the only sizable interior was the combined living and dining spaces, which, when the folding doors between them were open,

79. Arturo Bandini Bungalow, Pasadena, Calif.
Greene and Greene, Architects. *The House Beautiful*, June 1908.

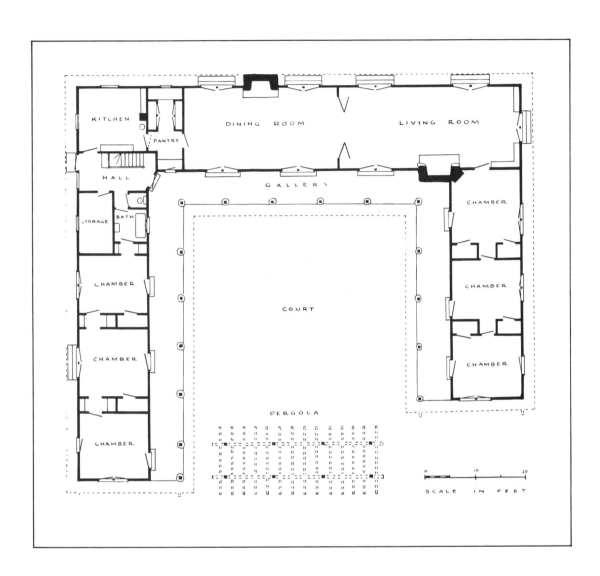

80. Plan of the Bandini Bungalow. Drawn by the author.

81. Interior of the Bandini Bungalow. View from dining toward living room. *House and Garden*, August 1907.

82. C. W. Hollister House and Floor Plan, Hollywood, Calif. Greene and Greene, Architects. *Country Life in America*, October 1906.

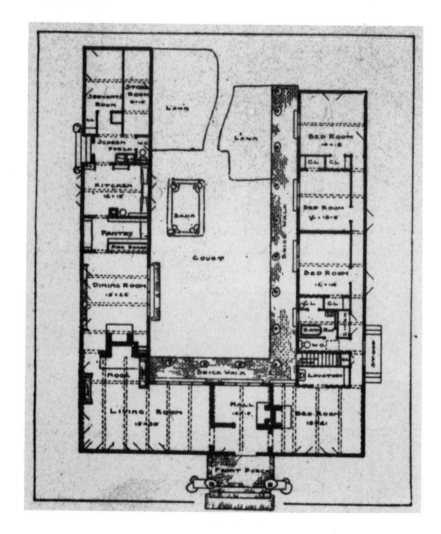

produced a sweep sixty-five feet long. On opposite long walls of each room was a cobblestone chimneypiece with a plain shelf over the fireplace.

Fig. 81

The Bandini bungalow has been demolished. The Greene brothers used something of its patio plan in the C. W. Hollister house at Hollywood, and (less so) in the Adelaide Tichenor house at Long Beach, both built soon afterward.

A photograph of the Hollister residence headed an important article attempting to elucidate the bungalow in *Country Life in America* in 1906. It was written by James M. A. Darrach, a practicing New York City architect, and was called "Why Not a Bungalow?" A subtitle characterizes it as: "THE SIMPLEST, MOST ECONOMICAL, AND ATTRACTIVE TYPE OF SMALL COUNTRY HOUSE." The author begins by tabulating the reasons why the bungalow was inexpensive to build and maintain. In condensed form they are:

Fig. 82

1. Being limited to a single story and having no stairs, which usually take up the space of a room on each floor, waste space is avoided.

2. Its basic simplicity and restful, horizontal lines make architectural ornament unnecessary.

3. Plumbing is concentrated on a single level.

4. Planning is such as to require few connecting corridors.

5. The form permits a minimum of labor in framing, and a maximum of ease in construction.

6. Heat does not escape to upper reaches, as there are none.

7. The interior, depending more on arrangement and proportion than on finish, can be executed simply.

Darrach speaks of the bungalow as lacking a stereotyped layout or form, and he introduces the idea that it is "a dwelling or shelter planned primarily to bring under roof the greatest number of the charms of the outdoor life—a house whose atmosphere is, as far as possible, that of the woods and fields." A bungalow is best suited to "a country whose temperature is uniformly warm," and its planning should take into consideration "the lay of the land, prevailing winds, means of approach, view, exposure with regard to the sun," and "windows should be considered more as frames for . . . attractive vistas, rather than . . . as merely openings for light." Verandas or porches "are the transitory space between the outdoors and indoors," and they should be near the ground, with easy access from inside, even to the point of omitting "the entire side-wall dividing the room from the porch, so that they may be one. There should also be more open communication between the different rooms of the bungalow than of the house, since in this way an effect of space and roominess can be had with the least amount of floor space." Rooms are classified as belonging to three zones: "the parts used during the day, such as halls, living-rooms, studios, porches, loggias, etc.; the bedrooms and bathrooms; and the kitchen and service portion. Of late the demand for a large and spacious living-room has been almost universal, and about this as a centre or axis the other parts are grouped." The plan of the Hollister bungalow is an excellent example of separating the three classes of rooms: the living room occupies most of the front pavilion; the dining room, kitchen, and servants' quarters occur in sequence in the adjoining ell; and bedrooms and bath are in the other wing. Darrach concludes with the observation: "On the Pacific Slope the bungalow has thrived and spread, and a local type of bungalow architecture has been developed there. While this type is particularly suited to the Pacific climate and landscape, it also offers many pertinent suggestions to Eastern builders."[4]

The Darrach analyses, added to the earlier Lazear quotation on its origin, give us a better concept of what the bungalow is or was. With illustrations of the Hollister residence included in the *Country Life in America* article, the wall fabric is seen to be no longer limited to vertical boards, since this example is faced with split redwood shakes. The third Greene-and-Greene early patio house mentioned, the Tichenor resi-

Figs. 83, 85 dence, has exposed-frame walls filled with clinker bricks. The bricks are hard-burned, irregular in shape, and often purplish in color; and with cobblestones they became a California-bungalow hallmark. The main portion of the Tichenor house, facing the ocean, is two-storied.

A third article serves to round out the proposition of the bungalow's characteristics. It is Arthur C. David's "An Architect of Bungalows in California." The "Architect" referred to (like Lazear's "great man") is a pair—the Greene brothers. David reiterates much that was in the two essays that have been cited. After discussing the bungalow interior, advising that it should make use of simple materials and "keep as far as

83. Adelaide M. Tichener Bungalow, Long Beach, Calif. Greene and Greene, Architects. View from Tea House into court during construction (1904). Copied from photo in Charles S. Greene Collection.

possible its natural texture and hue," he breaks new ground in pointing out: "The exterior, on the other hand, should not be made to count very strongly in the landscape. It should sink, so far as is possible, its architectural individuality and tend to disappear in its natural background. Its color, consequently, no matter whether it is shingled or clapboarded, should be low in key and should correspond to that of the natural wood. Its most prominent architectural member will inevitably be its roof, because it will combine a considerable area with an inconsiderable height, and such a roof must have sharp projections and cast heavy shadows, not only for the practical purpose of shading windows and piazzas, but for the aesthetic one of making sharp contrasts in line and shade to compensate for the moderation of color. Its aesthetic character will necessarily be wholly picturesque; and it should be both surrounded by trees and covered, so far as is convenient, with vines."[5]

The key to David's external attributes of the bungalow, that is, of its being subdued in color, dominated by the roof, and blended with planting, had been suggested earlier in the article when he stated: "We are aware that the American bungalow derives more of its characteristics from Japanese models than it does from buildings erected in tropical countries."[6] The matter about the roof is certainly Far Eastern, Chinese as well as Japanese. One may contrast the sophisticated Western classical building—its walls overspread with pilasters and entablatures, spotted with pedimented doors and windows, and rising above the cornice line to parapets and balustrades that mask the roof—to the Eastern emperor's palace, Buddhist temple, or Shintō shrine, which are first glimpsed from a distance as a roof form floating among the trees. This impression generally holds while approaching and entering such a building, at which time one grasps the relationship between inner volume and overhead covering. The roofed space affords much greater flexibility of arrangement than the walled space; it lends itself to the organic principle of the Chicago School (the principle that "form follows function"), which Frank Lloyd Wright "discovered" that the Chinese had known and used for upwards of two millenia upon reading Lao-tzu's *Tao-tê-ch'ing*.[7]

That the Greene brothers got details for their work from authentic Japanese sources is evident from the forms themselves. The architects never having been to Japan, their knowledge would have come from having seen the Hōōden at the Chicago fair, the structures in the Japanese Tea Garden at San Francisco (both visited en route to Southern California or soon afterward), or the large Japanese precinct at the Louisiana Purchase Exposition at Saint Louis in 1904,[8] or the forms may have been derived from pictures. Charles Sumner Greene still had stacks of mounted photographs in his Carmel studio during his late years.[9] The architects also must have had picture books. Edward S. Morse's *Japanese Homes and Their Surroundings*, published at Boston in 1886, with its more than three-hundred illustrations, has remained up to the present day the most authentic source on the subject in print. Otherwise unexplained features, such as posts resting on stones pounded into the earth, the projection of plates beyond gable bargeboards, and even walls of vertical boards with battens, as in the Bandini bungalow, are shown in the Morse book as proper to the Japanese dwelling. The Japanese house, like the colored woodblock print, was and had been for a long time a highly developed proletarian art, and as such it provided an apt model for a democratic society's housing needs.

Fig. 84

More assertive Japanese elements are to be seen in the Adelaide M.

84. Entrance to a House in Tokyo. E. S. Morse, *Japanese Homes and Their Surroundings*, Boston, 1886.

85. Watercolor Rendering of the Adelaide M. Tichenor Bungalow by Charles S. Greene. Courtesy of Greene and Greene Library, Pasadena, Calif.

86. Perspective of the Theodore M. Irwin House, Pasadena, Calif. Greene and Greene, Architects. Restored Drawing by the author.

Tichenor bungalow at Long Beach, which the Greenes began in 1904, although the design did not reach its final stage until the following year. The most distinct Japanese motif was not the rear courtyard (even with its arched bridge) but the main mass of the house. Its bank fenestration, horizontal balconies, corner accents (like rain-door boxes), and tile *irimoya* roof (were it not for the chimney) present a convincing Japanese impression.

Fig. 85

The first of the sizable Japanesque bungalows was a remodeled and enlarged house for Theodore M. Irwin at the corner of North Grand Avenue and Arroyo Terrace in Pasadena. Originally a spreading, single-storied, hipped-roofed house with open center court, built by the Greenes for Katherine M. Duncan in 1900,[10] it became completely two-storied around the open space six years later. The house was of timber construction, the walls were partly shingled, shaded by deep eaves of the low-pitched gabled roofs, with subtle curves, and the enveloping retaining walls, terraces, piers, and chimneys were of masonry, combining cobblestones and clinker bricks. A Japanese lantern and chimney caps of similar contours lent exotic touches. The curved terrace (with potted bay trees) reflects that of the Schweinfurth bungalow at Newton

Fig. 86

Fig. 87
Fig. 50,
Frontis.

Centre. The plan is one of the less successfully conceived by the Greenes, no doubt due to the differences in concept between the two stages of the house. An existing photograph of the 1900 version shows a driveway on the site of the later walk, which was to take a circuitous route to the hall portal. The lack of conspicuous entrance is Japanese, though rather confusing in an American house; and the separation of stairhall and reception hall (requiring passage through the living room and another room from one to the other) is decidedly awkward. The medley of small rooms to the south of the court must have been left over from the Duncan regime. A pool, fountain, seats, plants, and vine-covered trellis enhance the court. Living and dining rooms are wainscoted and have beamed ceilings. One of the pleasantest features is the new drive at the rear, winding up the slope and under the fan-shaped porte-cochere—expanding from a covered porch leading to the entry that opens into the court—with a paved motor area in front of the garage. Boulders are set by the parapet at the near side of the terrace to serve as steps over the wall to the driveway. Several of the upstairs

Fig. 88

87. The Irwin House from the Grand Avenue Entrance.
The Craftsman, August 1912.

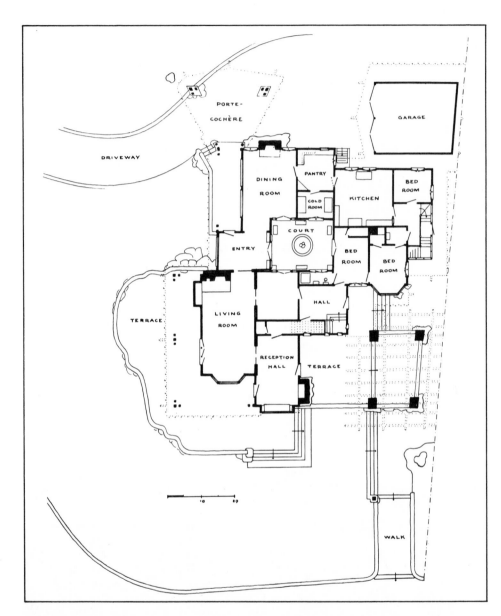

88. Restored First- and Second-floor (*opposite*) Plans of the Irwin House. Drawn by the author.

bedrooms are accessible only from the open gallery around the court. Bathrooms are plentifully supplied for a house of this period.

The apex of Greene and Greene's architectural achievements was attained in seven projects undertaken during 1907 through 1909. The first was what may be described as a monumental bungalow commissioned by Robert R. Blacker for the prestigious Oak Knoll subdivision in Pasadena. Blacker had approached Myron Hunt and Elmer Grey for designs, which were executed for a masonry mission-style house, but because of the San Francisco earthquake of 1906 they struck Blacker as unsafe. However, he liked their floor plan, and the Greene brothers adopted it for a wood building. The nucleus was a great stairhall, between *Figs. 89, 90* two parallel wings, which flowed into the living room at the front of one, and into the dining room, with "glass porch" beyond, at the rear of the other. A pergola extended on axis with the latter. To break the static look of a perfectly balanced front, a porch was attached to the

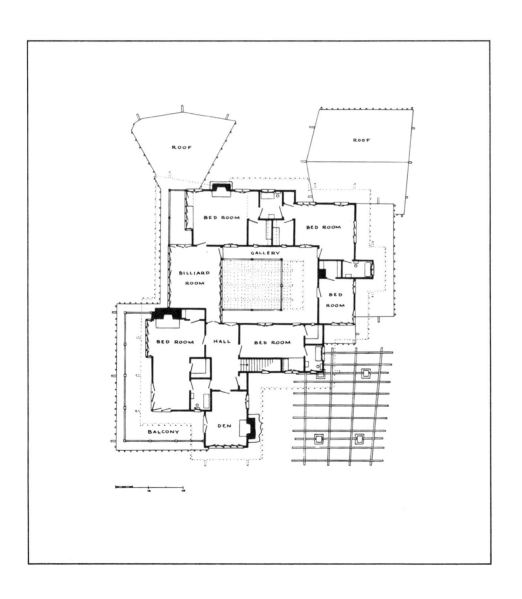

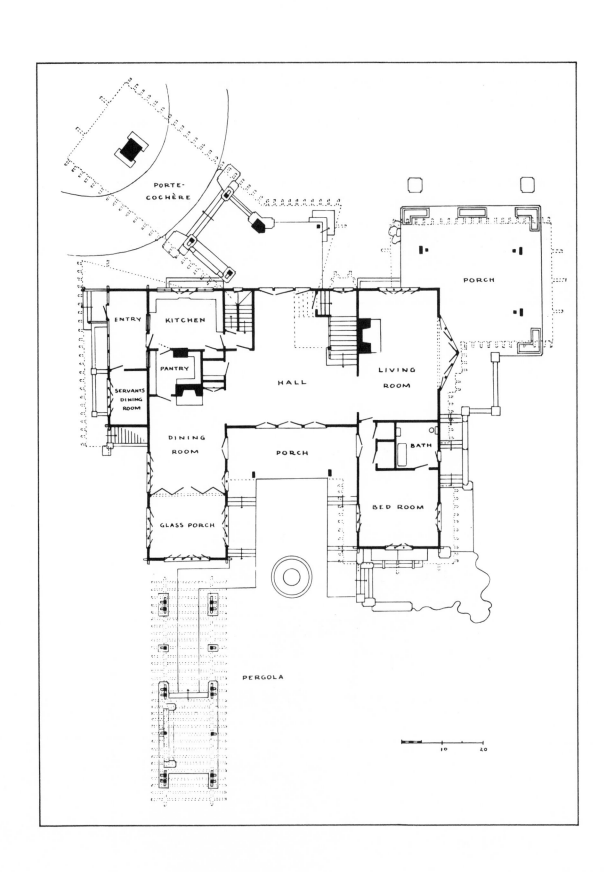

PORTE-
COCHÈRE

PORCH

ENTRY KITCHEN

PANTRY

LIVING
ROOM

SERVANTS
DINING
ROOM

HALL

DINING
ROOM

PORCH

BATH

BED ROOM

GLASS PORCH

PERGOLA

10   20

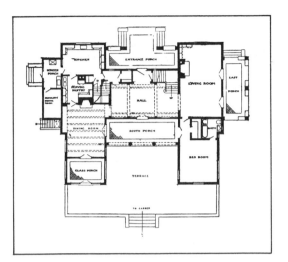

89–92. (*Opposite*) First-floor Plan of a House for R. R. Blacker, Pasadena. Greene and Greene, Architects. Drawn by the author. (*Left*) First-floor Plan of a House for R. R. Blacker, Pasadena. Hunt and Grey, Architects. *The Craftsman*, October 1907. (*Middle*) Front Elevation of the Blacker House. Greene and Greene, Architects. (*Below*) Porte-cochere Detail of the Blacker House. Photo 1954.

93. David B. Gamble Bungalow, Pasadena. Greene and Greene, Architects. Photo by Marvin Rand.

Fig. 91

Fig. 92

living-room corner, and a porte-cochere angled out in the other direction from the hall doors. This shelter over the turnaround is a remarkable structure, consisting of long, squared beams supporting a truss system for the joists of the flat roof, and resting on a single complex brick pier with stepped-out bracket-cantilevers of wood. Three large upper balconies offered vistas over the ample grounds, which were landscaped in the Japanese manner (Chapter Nine). This is the first house we have seen with considerable planting against the foundations of the building, which was innovative in the United States, and was to become a bungalow trademark.

Fig. 93

Fig. 94

A second masterwork of this era was the home of David B. Gamble, retired tycoon of the Proctor and Gamble Ivory Soap empire. It was on Westmoreland Place, overlooking the Arroyo, and not far from the Irwin house. The building bristles with rafter ends and much open timber-work to the porches; but the form avoids symmetry, divides into horizontal registers, and is surrounded by terraces. The interior space has a flow similar to that in the Blacker house, only both living and dining rooms are at the rear, to benefit from the view. The wood joinery, stained glass, metalwork, and specially woven rugs are worthy of the superb volume treatment.[11] Six bedrooms, three sleeping porches, and four-and-a-half baths are on the second floor, and a billiard room is on the third.

In 1966 the grandchildren of David B. Gamble bestowed his home upon the City of Pasadena, in a joint agreement with the University of Southern California, through its School of Architecture and Fine Arts, to become the Greene and Greene Library. It serves both as an archives and as a museum containing the original furnishings. It is remarkable that this, one of the largest houses examined, has most persistently kept its designation as a bungalow. It is listed on the National Register of Historic Buildings.

A third noteworthy specimen of the Greene brothers' apex seven is the home of Charles M. Pratt at Nordhoff, seventy-five miles northwest of Los Angeles, built in 1909. The Pratt bungalow is neither a large compact mass nor a courtyard house; it is a multi-angled crescent shape adjusted to its ridge site overlooking the Ojai Valley. The plan may have derived from a summer cottage designed by Katherine C. Budd, so laid out that "expensive grading [was] avoided and the protection of the

94. Panorama of Entrance Hall with Stairway, and Living Room, David W. Gamble House. Photo by Marvin Rand.

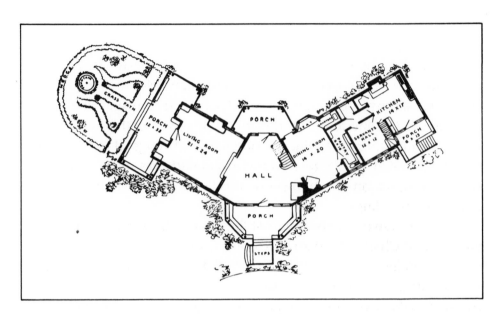

95. First-floor Plan of a Summer Cottage by K. C. Rudd.
Country Life in America, October 1903.

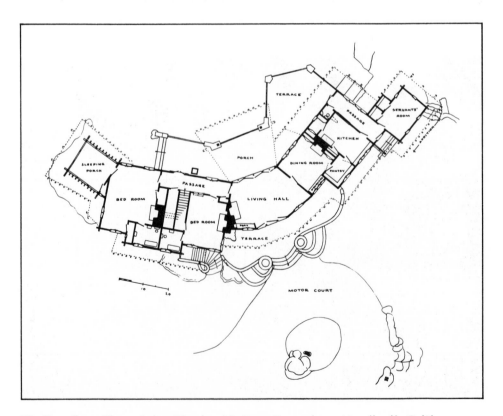

96. First-floor Plan of the Charles M. Pratt Bungalow, Nordhoff, Calif.
Green and Greene, Architects. Measured and drawn by the author.

hill-side secured."[12] Such an idea would have appealed to Charles S. and Henry M. Greene, and it would have been utilized where conditions called for it. The center of the Budd house is a wedge-shaped hall with stairway, corner fireplace, and polygonal porches front and back. Living and dining rooms beyond are in wings set at an obtuse angle to each other. The Pratt plan has no living room other than the wedge shape, and the stairway is located elsewhere. The earlier house has ample upstairs accommodations (seven chambers), whereas in the Pratt house one end pavilion is fully two-storied, and contains two sleeping apartments, two baths and a sleeping porch on each level. The remainder of the house is one-storied and swings away from the dormitory in a dynamic fashion, involving a series of changes in angle, curvilinear steps and stepped terraces—muffled with planting—and gables like flapping birds' wings. The timber treatment includes copper casings over protruding beam ends in the Japanese manner. Pebble-studded concrete chimney caps are more successful than the somewhat affected lantern type on the Irwin house. The meandering rear terrace, partly covered and affording spectacular views, spans the length of the bed-

Fig. 95

Fig. 96

Fig. 97

97. Entrance to the Charles M. Pratt Bungalow. Photo 1954.

room-pavilion passage, living hall, dining room, all the way to the service passage at the east end, an outdoor-living adjunct to the house. Even the motor court, with its boulder steps across from the front terrace, seems as much of an ambulatory facility as the graveled flats laid out around Baroque and Rococo princely dwellings in Europe. Inside the Pratt bungalow the space shifts with the wall angles. As in the Blacker and Gamble houses, here furniture and fittings were designed and their construction supervised by the architects (Chapter Eight).

Greene and Greene also engaged in small and sometimes prosaic little houses. One was an inexpensively built rental property for Josephine van Rossem near the Arroyo View reservoir. It was a two-storied, horizontally clapboarded house of three rooms, two porches, and a toilet downstairs, and four bedrooms and bathroom above, built in *Fig. 98* 1903.[13] Three years later it was renovated for a new owner, James W. Neill. Its only increase in size was the expansion of the living room into the area of the former porch, to be entered directly from a new portal, *Fig. 99* yet the change in appearance was drastic. It was costumed in shingles and timbers, with projecting beams to the bargeboards, and the doubled, single-paned sash windows became triple casements. Architectural landscaping included a terraced front yard retained by a beautifully conceived battered wall of boulders and clinker bricks, with a pergola spanning the brick-paved driveway. At some later date walls were

98. Sketch of the Josephine van Rossem Rental Cottage, Pasadena. Greene and Greene, Architects. Drawn by the author.

99. James W. Neill House, Pasadena. Greene and Greene, Architects.
Photo by Marvin Rand.

stuccoed and the arbor removed, but happily both features have been restored by the present owner and Greene and Greene authority, Randell L. Makinson.

There can be no question regarding the premier place held by Greene and Greene in the bungalow movement in California. Other architects worked in a similar vein, or even copied them, and some of their results received the Greene seal of approval. An article by Charles S. Greene, called "Impressions of Some Bungalows and Gardens," includes illustrations of several structures by Walker and Vawter of Los Angeles.[14] One is the rear of an unidentified bungalow, praised for its "placing . . . in relation to the sycamore trees. The harmony and picturesqueness are admirable." Greene comments that their work "attests the skill of the well-trained designer. The selection of materials is excellent. The harmony of split shakes and rough bricks is not to be questioned. The carefully rounded timbers and well-proportioned piers and buttresses combine the feelings of elegance, with adequate sense of support." One cannot miss the point that these are strong principles in the author's own work.

Fig. 100

100. Rear of Bungalow in Los Angeles. Walker and Vawter, Architects.
The Architect, December 1915.

101. Bungalow in Pasadena. John C. Austin, Architect. *The Western Architect*, June 1909.

Another specimen pictured in the same article was built in Pasadena in 1908 after a design by John C. Austin, although no such identification accompanied its photo. The little squarish building is flat-topped, and Charles Greene evaluated it as "a simple effective design with the exception of the projecting halved timbers, which is carried to a point of affectation." Another writer called it "a remarkably daring utilization of Japanese motives."[15] In all likelihood—rather than from any Japanese model—the interpretation of vertical and horizontal members derived from ancient wood dwellings in Lycia, Asia Minor. An essay on this subject, accompanied by a drawing of such a building restored from rock-cut sepulchral remains, was published shortly before Austin conceived the Pasadena house and may have suggested its image. The living room is at the front, dining room and kitchen are on the far side, and bedrooms are at the back of the bungalow. The chimney and adjacent porch were removed about 1950 and replaced by a broad deck over a carport.

Fig. 101

Fig. 102

The adaptability of the picturesquely composed frame bungalow, of shake-covered walls and low-pitched, deeply overhanging roof, to a

102. Restoration Drawing of an Ancient Dwelling in Lycia, Asia Minor. *American Architect and Building News*, 30 September 1908.

103. John T. Allen House at Hollywood. A. R. Kelly, Architect. *Country Life in America*, May 1914.

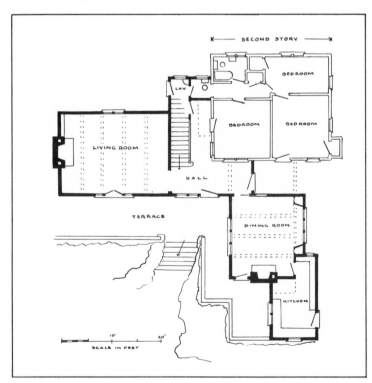

104. Floor Plans of the John T. Allen House. Drawn by the author.

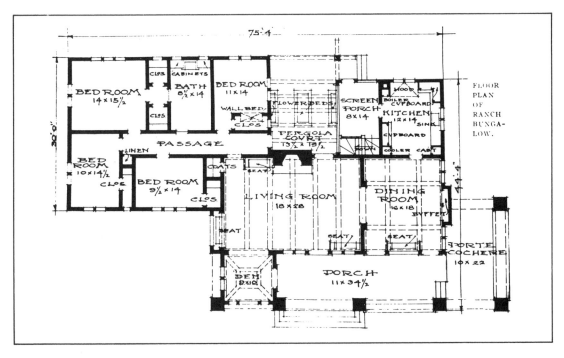

105, 106. Ranch Bungalow of J. C. McConnell near Burbank, Calif. Photograph and Floor Plan. Barnes and Rust, Architects. *The Craftsman*, May 1912.

rugged site is shown by the John T. Allen house at Hollywood; it was designed by Arthur R. Kelly and built before 1910. It was located on a steep and irregular hillside facing the valley, and following its front contour is a terrace with walls and parapets of boulders, creating an under space that served for storage. A stairhall and the three main rooms are on the principal floor; the second story is level with the

Fig. 103

Fig. 104

ceiling of the first, but no part is actually over it. The chamber story is built on its own foundations "at a higher level, a shelf having been cut out to receive it." The house literally has grown out of its site: "The rock used for the terrace walls was dug out of the hillside, and the whole color scheme of the house is such as to make it seem as though it had always belonged here." Its architect spoke of the building as being a "Swiss type."[16] The *Craftsman* declared: "Curiously enough, the effect of the building is more Japanese than Swiss"; and Henry Saylor labeled it a "ranch house."[17]

Figs. 105, 106

A "ranch bungalow"—so designated—stood on a forty-acre tract near Burbank. It was the home of rancher J. C. McConnell, and was designed by A. S. Barnes and E. B. Rust of Los Angeles. It looked like a suburban bungalow, being compact and having a porte-cochere at one end. A range of square brick piers spanned the front, and the bay farthest from the porte-cochere was enclosed for a den. Except for this extra little room the accommodations were equal to those of the Allen house, though all on one floor, and including a "pergola court" (in place of the terrace) back of the living room. Framing was exposed

107. Francis T. Underhill Bungalow, Santa Barbara, Calif.
Country Life in America, November 1915.

108. Dining Room in the Underhill Bungalow. *Country Life in America*, November 1915.

inside, with brackets partly arching openings; the main rooms had tray, beamed ceilings, and furniture was in the mission manner.

One of the most casual of early-twentieth-century bungalows in California was built by "intuition" on the part of its owner, who lacked training in architecture. He was Francis T. Underhill of Santa Barbara, and his home was called "La Chiquita." Originally it was a simple rectangular shape covered by a low-pitched hipped roof. A Los Angeles architect remarked about it that if the house "had a thatched roof, one would not have to use any imagination to feel that it was the real Indian bungalow."[18] As one can see, the walls were mostly fenestration, the windows varied, and stepped forward and back under the eaves. A sense of wall was achieved by heavy muntins, except in the dining room, where most of the two outer sides were single panes of plate glass, giving the impression of dining out-of-doors. Date palms on the window ledge and a beamed ceiling overhead went with the heavy mission furniture. By 1915, when this picture was published, the Underhill bungalow had acquired an addition, giving it an L shape. La Chiquita had appeared in color on the cover of the September, 1914, issue of *Country Life in America*, whose theme was "All about Bungalows," and it

Fig. 107

Fig. 108

109. Clapboarded Bracketed Bungalow, San Diego, Calif. Photo 1954.

figured among "The Best Twelve Country Houses in America," chosen by bungalow authority Henry H. Saylor, in his article in the November, 1915, edition of the same periodical.

In contrast to the sophisticated examples (which includes the Underhill house) that we have examined, most of which were on ample sites, there were other bungalows that were less pretentious, and most of them were situated on restricted lots. Builders of the first group were more or less familiar with the ideals of the movement, and they were inspired accordingly. Builders of the second tended more to take features from the first and incorporate them without real understanding. Most of these builders started with the handicap of a dull, flat, little lot, hemmed in by monotonous neighbors; and they can be forgiven for their efforts in attempting to infuse a little character into their work. For a glimpse of this reverse-side-of-the-bungalow coin, let us consider several small early-twentieth-century dwellings in San Diego.

Fig. 109   The first is a minimal residence of traditional (non-bungalow) materials. Although the chimney bricks are not of the California clinker variety, at least the clapboard siding has been stained, not painted.

Eaves are thin and wide, and they are supported by prominent braces. The form is narrow but deep, and with the roof sloping front and back the long plane is relieved by a slight dip and two penetrating gables. A bay window beyond the external chimney breaks up the side wall. The small window in the gable indicates that the second level was only used for storage.

The second house—abandoned at the time it was photographed— probably is the earliest of the set. Its chimneys still retain late-nineteenth-century ("Queen Anne") caps. It is sheathed in thin boards; its roof *Fig. 110* rafters are thin, too, and rounded at the eaves' end. A great curled projection comes out of the corner of the belvedere or clerestory set on the dipping hipped roof. The pent-and-gable roof over the arch of the recessed entrance, flanked by square windows, is inviting. The propped-up bay window adjoining appears an afterthought. Although without surrounding galleries, the house repeats the shape of a contemporary peristyle bungalow at Palm Springs,[19] thus keying in with some of the early East Coast bungalows.

The third also is clapboarded, and it has roof flares, wide eaves, and open timberwork. Like the first San Diego example, there is an external *Fig. 111*

110. Hipped-roofed Bungalow with Clerestory, San Diego. Photo 1954.

111. Bungalow with Gabled Dormer Windows, San Diego. Photo 1954.

brick chimney; but it misses the other's bungalow feeling, because of the upward thrust of elements: the roof pitch is too steep, and the coverings of the dormers are set unnecessarily high, with blank spaces above the windows. Porch, parapet, posts, and trim are matter-of-factly conceived. It is difficult to detect the design roots of this house, but they certainly are not ranch-house, chalet, or Japanese. Perhaps there is a bit of Hudson River bracketed (the brackets played down). The shape of the front gables hint at a type favored by Calvert Vaux, upturned at the bases, though Vaux's invariably had cutout bargeboards.[20] In all probability neither the builder nor the client gave the matter much thought. It is a folk bungalow.

The fourth in the San Diego group best shows the bungalow characteristics of horizontality, timber and clinker-brick construction, and *Fig. 112*   prickly details. It is unfortunate that the wood members have been painted white, and probably this was a recent disfigurement. The proper element beautifully maintained here is the planting, consisting of evergreens and shrubs set near to the house, with due consideration for corner accents. The greenery composes with the bungalow and affords its occupants a measure of privacy.

Japanese elements, such as were used with restraint in the last example, could get out of hand easily, as in the Alvord house in Brooklyn, which, it will be recalled, was motivated for lucrative returns. The California equivalent was created by the De Luxe Building Company of Los Angeles. An early version, pictured in the *Bungalow Magazine* in 1914, was captioned: "This Type of Bungalow One Would Wager is the Design of a True Japanese."[21] Later simplified (the original had white boulders set at the corners of all masonry forms, dark elsewhere), a new element had been discerned in its flying eaves, and the design henceforth was an "Aeroplane Bungalow" with "Japanese Architectural Detail."[22] The elements are exceedingly busy: the roof is complicated unnecessarily, pavilions jut out without reason, and materials shift every few feet from cobblestones to shingles to timberwork. The plan, however, is fairly simple, with a living room (15-by-30 feet) across the front, expanding into one corner flanker as an inglenook, and into the other as a music retreat. Columns are in the opening to the dining room behind, and a small breakfast room is to one side. At the back are kitchen, maid's room, and two other bedrooms and bath. The square upper story con-

Fig. 58

Fig. 113

112. A Low-lying Bungalow with Authentic Planting, San Diego. Photo 1954.

tains a small sewing room, three bedrooms, closets, two sleeping porches, and a bath. The "aeroplane"-Japanese-style bungalows bring to mind the Airship Building at Dreamland, the Coney Island amusement park, as well as Wright's house for E. A. Gilmore at Madison.

The subdivision massing of bungalows and the mass production of bungalows (harking back to the earliest English "portable" bungalows) led to the bungalow court, which was a precinct containing a number of rentable dwellings built by a single owner. Although a commercial venture, there were a number of good features. In the first place it offered a more desirable atmosphere than an apartment building, as each unit was detached, giving it privacy, and there was attractive planting around it. Each was scaled to the individual and to the small family. Children had a place to play outdoors. Often the scheme included an outdoor gathering place for grownups, which was especially appreciated by mothers and nurses, who could visit with each other and watch their charges at the same time. With the increasing use of private automobiles, the bungalow court was a haven that excluded through traffic, though it provided a place for parking cars owned by the tenants. As opposed to the normal subdivision, where various clients built different and often inharmonious houses side by side, in the bungalow court

113. "Aeroplane" Bungalow Built by the De Luxe Building Company, Los Angeles. *Bungalow Magazine*, August 1916.

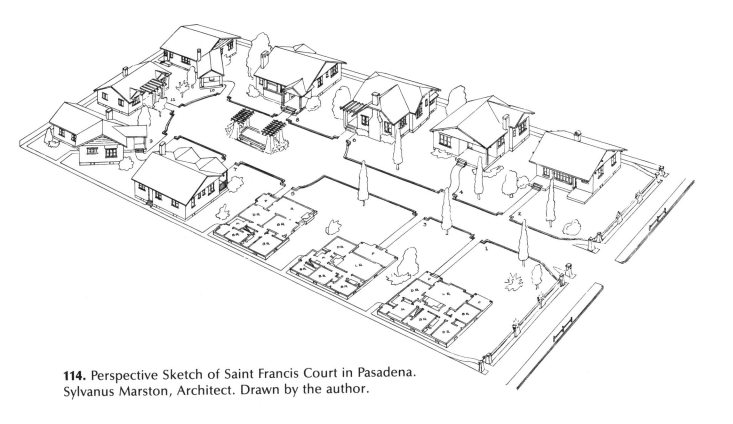

114. Perspective Sketch of Saint Francis Court in Pasadena.
Sylvanus Marston, Architect. Drawn by the author.

everything from the overall landscaping to the component bungalow
was planned by the same architect, which fostered unity throughout.
Because there was no private ownership, there were no property-line
fences or other separations; the natural setting flowed around each
bungalow. The court concept probably grew out of earlier summer-
cottage rentals, such as Edward F. Underhill conducted at Nantucket,
only the California bungalow version was a year-round enterprise. It
was the poorer man's Llewellyn Park.

    An attractive example of such a bungalow community was Saint
Francis Court in Pasadena, designed by Los Angeles architect Sylvanus
Marston only two or three years after having graduated from the Cornell
University architectural program in 1907. Along the street front was
built a boulder wall having post accents at the entrances, with brick
copings and other decorations, and attached lighting fixtures. Saint
Francis Court covered a rectangular site of 176 by 305 feet, with a 20-foot
drive down the center, expanding to a sort of plaza with an architectural
motif in the center, which consisted of a fountain pool with benches
along the sides, and a cobblestone-piered pergola having planting at
each end. The court contained eleven frame bungalows, differing in

Fig. 42

Fig. 114

shape and materials (walls were shingled, clapboarded, or plastered, with exposed timbers), but of similar size, and covered by wide roofs of uniform pitch. Plans varied, but each contained a living room (averaging 15-by-20 feet), dining room (averaging 12-by-15 feet), kitchen (averaging 8-by-12 feet), three bedrooms (averaging 12-by-12 feet), closets, bath-room, and cellar. Living rooms had beamed ceilings and brick fireplaces, some of them in inglenooks. A service walk encircled the court for back-door deliveries to all of the bungalows. Today, Robinson's Depart-ment Store occupies the site.[23]

Fig. 166

A larger development of the same sort was Bowen's Court, designed by Arthur B. Heineman of Pasadena. Its layout extended along two narrow strips at right angles, with a Japanese garden arranged around a fish pond at the junction. The twenty-three bungalows, eleven of which

115. Advertisement for Bungalow Plans by F. G. Brown of Los Angeles. *The House Beautiful,* May 1908.

116. Ralph N. Maxson Bungalow, Lexington, Ky. F. G. Brown, Architect. Photo *ca.* 1910, Courtesy of Mrs. Jessie T. Maxson.

were two-family houses, were accessible only on foot. Units were smaller than those in Saint Francis Court, having combined living and dining rooms, a kitchen, and two bedrooms. Rent was $25 a month unfurnished, or from $30 to $75 a month furnished.[24]

The multiplication of bungalows by California architects was not limited to the state or even to the West Coast. The medium for the dissemination was printed plans, which were advertised in the home magazines of the period, and ranged from a leaflet costing a few cents to a book. In one issue of *House Beautiful*, for instance, are three Los Angeles concerns' advertisements. E. W. Stillwell offered the booklets: *Representative California Homes*, 50¢; *West Coast Bungalows*, 50¢; and *Builder's Supplement*, 10¢. Ye Planry Building Company had a *Bungalow Book* of one hundred plans for 36¢. And the Bungalow Company presented the third edition of *California Bungalow Homes* for $1.00, as well as thirty-six *Model Bungalow Plans* for 25¢.[25]

This is how the phenomenon worked: Professor and Mrs. Ralph N. Maxson, of Lexington, Kentucky, ran across an advertisement by F. G.

Fig. 115   Brown in the May, 1908, issue of *House Beautiful*. His book and a portfolio of twenty-four designs sold for a dollar, which would be deducted from the purchase price of any measured drawings ordered. The Maxsons liked the bungalow illustrated, got the drawings, and had

Fig. 116   a local builder erect their house in Transylvania Park. The plan was reversed, so that the porch would extend on the right instead of the left side, and the living room, intended to span the entire front of the house, was divided by a partition with sliding doors, making a small study at the fireplace end, where Professor Maxson could interview

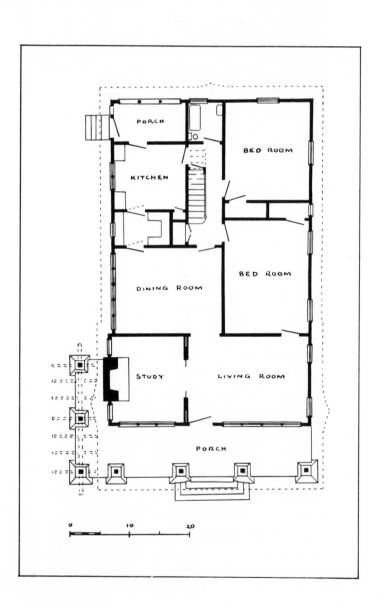

117. Plan of the Maxson Bungalow. Measured and drawn by the author.

students. The plan included a stairway to the second floor, where later *Fig. 117* the Maxsons finished several bedrooms. The flaring Japanesque lines were unique in the Southern environment where Colonial Revival houses were the accepted mode. The architect of the plan stated that ten years' experience in the Eastern states qualified him "to prepare specifications and make structural details suitable for building these houses in cold as well as in warm climates." This was an important factor in Kentucky, which, although Southern by virtue of its being below the Ohio River, nevertheless gets much of its winter weather directly from the Great Lakes.

California produced the widest range of bungalows of any state in America. In it was enacted the nearest thing to a full architectural evolution from the simplest rudimentary shelter (the barn) up to the most sophisticated manifestation. Its achievement was recognized abroad. The nation looked to California for guidance. It patronized its output. Not alone did California shine in individual bungalows but in the aggregate bungalow scene. Whether in luxury districts like Oak Knoll and Westmoreland Place or in lower-middle-income compounds like Saint Francis and Bowen's courts, artistry shaped the total environment. California pronounced just about the last word in the bungalow oration. The only notable utterance that could be added is tangent to the main vortex, and will be taken up next.

NOTES

1. From *Wasp*. Marion Randall Parsons, *Old California Homes*, Berkely, 1952, p. 118.

2. M. H. Lazear, "The Evolution of the Bungalow," *House Beautiful*, June 1914, p. 2.

3. Randell L. Makinson, *Greene & Greene, Architecture as a Fine Art*, Salt Lake City and Santa Barbara, 1977, pp. 42–53, 64–67.

4. James M. A. Darrach, "Why Not a Bungalow?" *Country Life in America*, October 1906, pp. 637–640.

5. Arthur C. David, "An Architect of Bungalows in California," *Architectural Record*, October 1906, p. 310.

6. *Ibid.*, p. 309.

7. Frank Lloyd Wright, *An Autobiography*, New York, 1942, pp. 196–197.

8. Charles went to St. Louis at the insistence of his client, Mrs. A. M. Tichenor, to look at wood displays and other items at the fair. Makinson, *op. cit.*, p. 98.

9. Clay Lancaster, "My Interviews with Greene and Greene," *Journal of the American Institute of Architects*, July 1957, p. 204.

10. Makinson, *op. cit.*, photograph p. 56.

11. The stained glass, notably the tree-of-life motif in the front doors, was designed by Charles S. Greene and executed by Emile Lange from carefully selected pieces in the Tiffany studio in New York.

12. Frances Phillips, "The Story of a Bungalow . . . Novel Treatment of a Typical Hillside Problem," *Country Life in America*, October 1903, p. 412.

13. Mackinson, *op. cit.*, p. 75.

14. *The Architect*, December 1915, pp. [258–259].

15. *House and Garden*, June 1916, p. 209.

16. Arthur R. Kelly, "California Bungalows," *Country Life in America*, May 1914, p. 82.

17. *The Craftsman*, October 1910, p. 86; Henry H. Saylor, *Bungalows*, Philadelphia, 1911, p. [82].

18. Kelly, *op. cit.*, p. 44.

19. "A Home in the Desert," *Country Life in America*, June 1911, p. 76.

20. Calvert Vaux, *Villas and Cottages*, New York, 1857, figures 1–2, p. 99; figures A, B, C, p. 92; Designs 6, 7, 12, 18, 19, 22, 24, 26, and 29.

21. "The Orient and Bungalow Types," *Bungalow Magazine*, April 1914, p. 246.

22. The full title of the article on it is: "Japanese Architectural Detail Copied in Aeroplane Bungalow Built at Los Angeles, California," *ibid.*, August 1916, pp. 489–491.

23. As built, St. Francis Court was somewhat simpler than as planned in the original drawings. For instance, the stone-piered porch support to bungalow no. 7 was changed to a wood post, and the three-part telescopic roof to bungalow no. 2 became a single roof. Marston's drawings are reproduced in Robert Winter, *The California Bungalow*, Los Angeles, 1980, p. 59. See others on pp. 25, 60, and 70. The perspective sketch here illustrated is compiled from plans and photographs in Henry H. Saylor, *Bungalows*, Philadelphia, 1911, pp. 20, 21, 22, 23, 24, 25, and 77.

24. Louis D. P. Millar, "The Bungalow Courts of California, Bowen's Court," *House Beautiful*, November 1916, pp. 338–339.

25. *Ibid.*, June 1912, pp. *vi*, *vii*.

VI

SPECIALIZED TYPE
BUNGALOWS

THE BUNGALOW, as defined in California, was the attainment of the American ideal in domestic building: it suited a democratic society, and it was conceived in a free and unrestrained manner. But also the term applied to buildings in which restrictions played an important role; they were of form, the most obvious having to do with architectural style. In the United States (unlike in England and elsewhere) these examples are legitimate bungalows, because the bungalow was a period movement, begun and accumulating momentum during the last two decades of the nineteenth century, fully flowering throughout the first quarter of the twentieth century, and slowly expiring over the next ten years. Any residence built during its heyday qualified as a bungalow. The last example illustrated in the proceding chapter is a "California" bungalow east of the Mississippi River. It has simply drifted away from the main channel that gushed out of the soil and flowed through California. In this chapter we shall examine a number of *period* bungalows that are not *definition* bungalows at all. They are rebels to the cause; or, inasmuch as the bungalow movement itself was rebellious, perhaps it would be better to characterize them as loyalist to one of a number of old regimes. In any event they are specialized types, without which our bungalow presentation would not be complete.

The first example can be identified only as having been "planned for a man of moderate wealth, who, while wishing to get away from the conventionalities and restrictions of city life, had the intention of 'roughing it' in comparative comfort, and of keeping his bungalow well filled for a great part of the year with young and lively company."[1] This libertine's retreat resembles Nathan Dunn's residence at Mount Holly in its pavilion layout and porch connecting the flankers. It belies the bungalow image in its steep roofs, and in its symmetry and formality. The last seems at odds with the intended purpose, which, however, is patently apparent in the bunk cells in each semi-detached wing, in the built-in lounging seats in the living-room inglenook, and in recesses of the veranda, the one next to the kitchen evidently for outdoor dining. The owner's comfort is assured by the bedrooms in the main pavilion, separated from the living room, and in having lavatory facilities well

Fig. 26
Fig. 118

118. Perspective and Inglenook Sketches, Front Elevation and Plan (*opposite*) of a Bungalow Retreat. *The Brickbuilder*, March 1908.

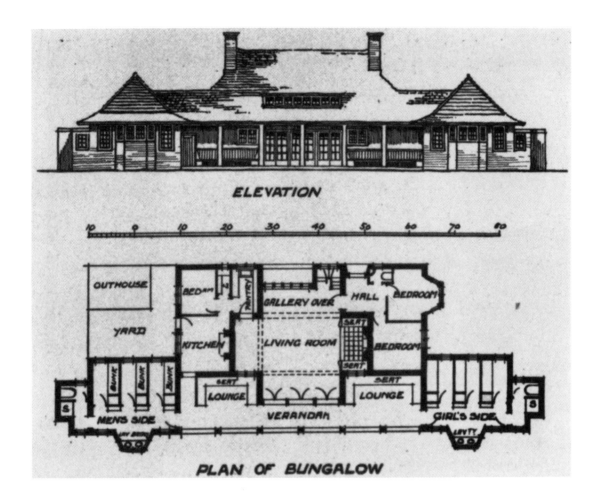

ELEVATION

PLAN OF BUNGALOW

distributed. The general effect is reminiscent of the East Indian caravanserai bungalow.

We have noted similarities between the Asian archetype and Spanish adobe houses in the New World, which contributed to early Greene and Greene bungalow originals. The feature avoided was the heavy walls. A contemporary to the Bandini bungalow was the Elbert Hubard residence near Santa Fe, New Mexico, making use of adobe-brick walls 16 inches thick. It was designed by V. O. Wallingford and built on a leveled hill site overlooking the city. It faces north, and has a gallery, "outdoor room," and *placeta* to trap the sun on the south. The scarcity of openings and brackets atop posts to the *portales* recall features in the seventeenth-century Palace of the Governors in Santa Fe. The plan also shows affinities. Both have projections at either end of the rear; rooms vary considerably in size, but are limited to full or half depth, and there

Figs. 22, 23, 24

Figs. 79, 80, 81, 82, 83

Fig. 119

Figs. 120, 121

119. Elbert Hubard Adobe
House, Santa Fe, N.M.
V. O. Wallingford, Architect.
House Beautiful, June 1907.

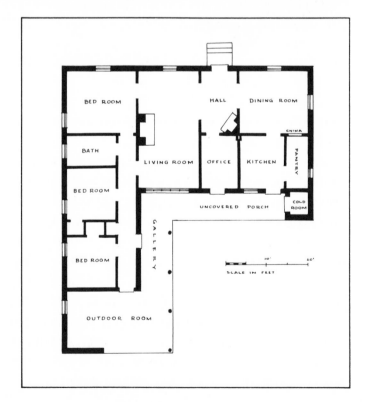

120. Floor Plan of the Elbert
Hubard Adobe House.
House Beautiful, June 1907.
Redrawn by the author.

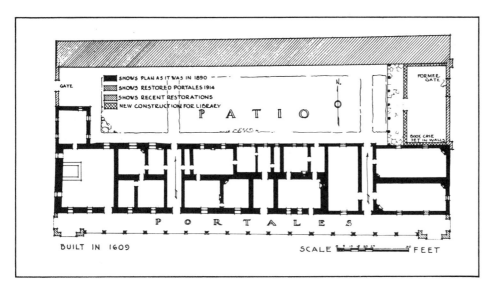

121. Floor Plan of the Palace of the Governors, Santa Fe. Rexford Newcomb, *Spanish Colonial Architecture in the United States*, New York, 1937.

are small corner fireplaces. However, partitions in the twentieth-century version have half the magnitude of the outer walls: that is, they are one rather than two adobe bricks in thickness. The low form, hipped roof, stuccoed walls, and simplified openings reflect elements of Gandy's attached cottages.

Fig. 8

A model for a specialized bungalow was offered by another Mediterranean type, this one considerably older than the Spanish, and from the middle or far end of that sea. It was the Hellenistic-Roman peristyle house, only this peristyle referred to a ring of columns around an inner courtyard rather than on the outside of the house. Such domiciles may be found at Pompeii, Priene, and Delos. The exterior of the house was plain, having walls unbroken except for a few doors; but it might be surrounded by shops, which had nothing to do with the house behind the walls. Rooms of the residence opened exclusively into the court. The shingled home of Mrs. James H. Codman at Wareham, Massachusetts, by architect Guy Lowell, except for having windows piercing the outer walls was almost as severe as the Mediterranean model. In the center was a square peristyle of twelve fluted Tuscan columns on high plinths or pedestals. One entered it from a front portico through an arched vestibule. The ten bedrooms (four for servants) at front and sides, and the living and dining rooms at the back were accessible only

Fig. 122

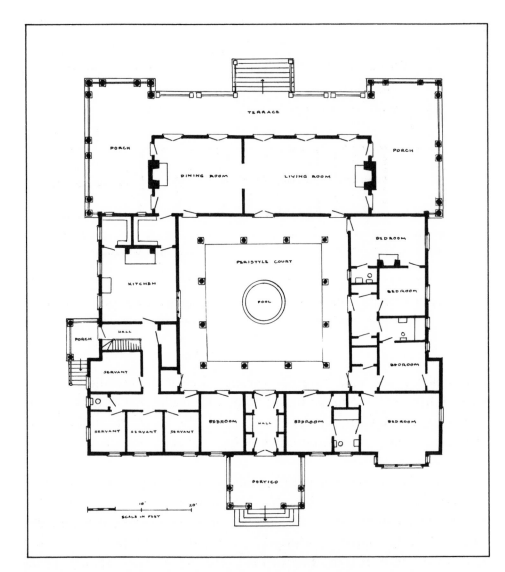

122. Floor Plan of Mrs. James M. Codman House, Wareham, Mass. Guy Lowell, Architect. Drawn by the author.

from the peristyle. Living and dining porches were beyond the two rooms, the last near the kitchen. The courtyard contained a circular pool, and symmetrical planting. Bungalow critic Henry Saylor labeled it a "patio bungalow."[2]

Figs. 123, 124, 125   A more compromising interpretation was a design published in *The Craftsman* during the year 1904. The house is shingled and hipped roofed, like Mrs. Codman's; but its peristyle court is open at the rear.

123. Perspective of a Rustic Peristyle-court Bungalow Design.
The Craftsman, July 1904.

124. View into the Peristyle-court of the Rustic Bungalow.
The Craftsman, July 1904.

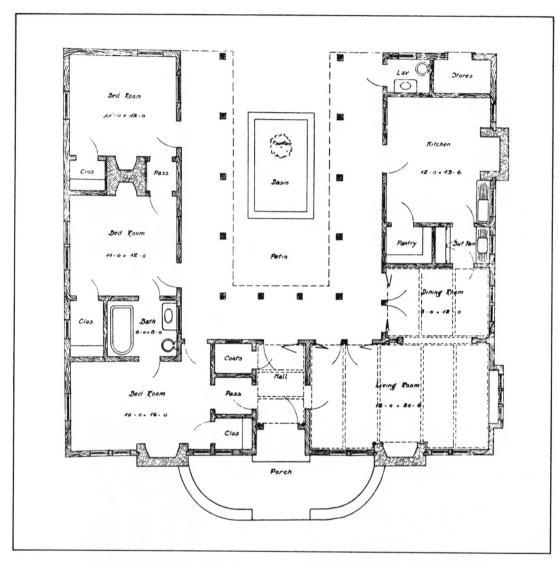

125. Floor Plan of the Rustic Peristyle-court Bungalow. *The Craftsman,* July 1904.

An attempt has been made to render it rustic by the use of twin boulder chimneys, the forms of which curve into parapets embracing an uncovered front porch. Accommodations are only a fraction of those of the Massachusetts house; the living-dining-kitchen arrangements occupy one side, and three bedrooms and bath the other. The rusticity extends into the court as a flagstone-paved area, where the columns are stripped-down tree trunks, with simple abacus capitals supporting a lintel. Beams run from it to the walls, and a flat ceiling extends outward as deep eaves. A pool (of different shape in plan and perspective) occupies the center and contains a fountain. It seems that the intermediary Spanish patio house makes a more acceptable model for the bungalow than the sophisticated antique domus, prompting incongruous modifications, as here.

Another building type introduced to the United States by continental Europeans is the log house, discussed in Chapter Two, and both early (eighteenth century) and revival (mid nineteenth century) examples are illustrated. Building with logs remained an ideal method for the remote lodge up into the bungalow period. A "log camp" summer home was built at White Bluffs, Tennessee, around the turn of the century. Though notched in the traditional saddle-joint manner, spruce logs laid horizontally for the walls were seasoned with the bark left on them, though they were "hand scraped to make a suitable inside finish."[3] Black mortar between the timbers was "scratched to give a shadow effect" on the exterior, and tinted to blend with the exposed wood within. Red cedar was employed for the rustic posts and railings of the

Figs. 19,
34, 35

Fig. 126

126. Log Camp at White Bluffs, Tenn. *The Western Architect*, October 1907.

127. Jack Ramsbottom House, Chestnut Hill, Mass. M. R. L. Freshel, Designer; J. E. Chandler, Architect. *The American Architect*, December 1904.

porch, doors, and roof shakes. A hipped roof is unique on a log house, and dormer windows at either end make possible a large (16-by-33-foot) dormitory upstairs. The first-story plan consisted of a long combined living and dining hall down the middle, flanked by four nearly square rooms, one a kitchen and the others bedrooms. There also were an enclosed stairway up to the dormitory, and a recessed back porch, with a small pantry at one corner and bathroom at the other. The log bungalow cost $1,800 to build.

As we have seen, log-house construction was brought to America by the Swedes before the middle of the seventeenth century. They later built more-permanent buildings of masonry, though these are without strong Swedish characteristics. The appearance of an authentic Scandinavian design awaited the bungalow period. Of Norwegian style, it was planned by Emarel Freshel and built in 1902 for Jack Ramsbottom, who was to be Mrs. Freshel's neighbor in Chestnut Hill, Massachusetts.[4] Working drawings were made by architect Joseph Everett Chandler, who chose to call it a Cottage in Norwegian Style. Foundations were of boulders, and chimneys of brick. Exterior walls were of flat, overlapping logs laid horizontally below, and vertical flush boards above, with cut-

Fig. 127

out design at the bottom of the overhanging planks. Turned posts were fitted on the corners, and were freestanding in the porches. Barge-boards were exceedingly deep, with apex finials, or the raking boards were crossed, as over the entrance porch. The front door opened into an L-shaped vestibule, with a staircase rising in the projection, and a fireplace backed up against that in the living room adjoining. The dining room beyond faced the lake in back, and its fireplace was at the far end. A secondary entrance in front led to a kitchen—or perhaps a study. The house has been degutted at this level for a large assembly hall. It and the Freshel Elizabethan house next door are now part of Boston College, called Philomatheia Hall and the Alumni House.

Similar to the Norwegian house but far from unique in the United States is the Swiss chalet type. We have seen such designs in Downing's *Architecture of Country Houses* as early as 1850. The style influenced *Figs. 31, 32* many of the buildings at the Philadelphia Centennial, and some of the lesser exhibits (such as the Idaho State Building) at the Chicago Colum-bian Exposition. As in the Allen house at Hollywood, critics saw chalet *Fig. 103* characteristics in California bungalows. Articles were devoted to this subject, as the imprint was apparent not only in the work of Arthur R. Kelly, and Greene and Greene, but in that of Myron Hunt, Elmer Grey, Louis Christian Mullgardt, Bernard Ralph Maybeck, Frank May, and Willis Polk.[5] Still, the authentic and high-styled Swiss house was rare. The outstanding American example is the A. D. Fisher residence in Walnut Hills, a suburb of Cincinnati. Commission for the house was given to Lucien F. Plympton, who is said to have married a Swiss woman and established connections in Switzerland. This renders plausible the claim that the elaborately shaped brackets, ornamental eaves, corbel tables, cutout designs, and other decorations of the house were fabricated in the Alps and assembled on the site in 1892. The first story of the Fisher *Fig. 128* chalet is only about 30-by-40 feet in plan, including the front porch, but the house is large, being four-and-a-half-storied at the rear because of the site decline. The layout is odd. The living hall, entered directly from the porch, contains a curvilinear stairway, and about half of the first-story ceiling is cut away as an open well. The room is amply lighted by *Fig. 129* fenestration both above and below the balcony at the head of the stairs. A reception nook is alongside the front porch, and the dining room is behind, with French doors opening onto the side balcony. The kitchen at present is in the overhanging pent at the back, but originally it was in the little room with the big fireplace adjoining. Windows are case-

128. A. D. Fisher Chalet,
Walnut Hills, Cincinnati, Ohio.
L. F. Plympton, Architect.
Inland Architect, January 1897.

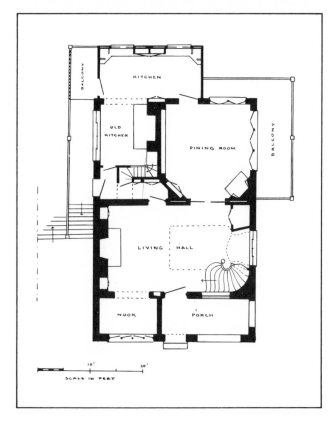

129. First-floor Plan of the A. D.
Fisher Chalet. Measured and
drawn by the author.

130. View of the Imperial Japanese Garden from the Observation Wheel,
Saint Louis, Mo. D. R. Francis, *The Universal Exposition of 1904*,
Saint Louis, 1913.

ments, hinged or sliding. The porch has been enclosed to match the
reception nook.

Another importation, which served a different purpose before assum-
ing a permanent role as a bungalow, came from Japan. Initially it was
part of the Imperial Japanese Garden at the Louisiana Purchase Exposition held in Saint Louis during 1903–04. As in Chicago and San Francisco,
the official architecture of the early-twentieth-century fair was a monumental style, in this case Baroque, whose splendor outshone both of its
predecessors. The Nipponese display again stood out from the rest of
the halls by virtue of its difference in character. At the main gate stood
the Formosa Pavilion (Formosa, now Taiwan, then being under Japanese
dominion); to the right was the commissioners' office, and behind it, in
the corner of the precinct, was the bazaar, where things made in Japan
were sold. In the hollow, by the pond, was the Golden Pavilion, a
reproduction of the three-storied Kinkaku built at the end of the four-
teenth century, near Kyoto. Up the hill was the Main Pavilion, a reduced
version of the Shishinden (Purple Dragon Hall), the reception hall of the
eighth-century Imperial Palace at Heian-ko (Kyoto). Near it stood the

Fig. 130

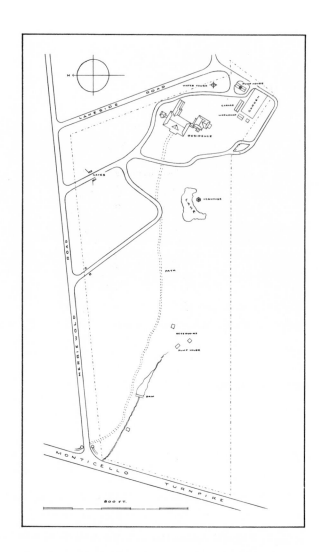

131. Plan of the Shō-fu-den Residence Lot, Merriewold Park, near Monticello, N.Y. Drawn by the author.

Fig. 131

little Bellevue, which had been a pavilion at the Osaka Exposition held the previous year.

At the conclusion of the Louisiana Purchase Exposition some of the architectural and other embellishments of the Imperial Japanese Garden were given to an eminent Japanese scientist, Dr. Jokichi Takamine, who had made his home in the United States.[6] They were taken to and set up on his estate at Merriewold Park, a few miles south of Monticello, New York, to become his summer residence. Dr. Takamine called it Shō-fu-den, Pine-Maple Hall, after the indigenous trees. The buildings were assembled on a rocky rise farthest from the road. The former Main Pavilion became the nucleus, facing northwest; the commissioners' office

132. Shō-fu-den from the West. Photo 1954.

133. Dining Room at Shō-fu-den. Photo 1954.

was attached by a pergola or covered passage at the south corner, as a bedroom wing; and the little Bellevue was similarly appended on the northeast flank, as a reception room. The gates to the principal entrance of the Imperial Garden were set up on the drive nearest the house. A service wing was added at the rear of the main pavilion; and garage, workshops, gardener's dwelling, ice, spring, and pump houses were built off to the south. Over a ten-year period the estate was enlarged to fifteen hundred acres. A boat house on the lake and various farm buildings were erected in Japanese style.[7]

Fig. 132

The principal external change to the main pavilion was an extension at the front of the roof to shelter the porch steps. With its perimeter galleries and deeply overhanging eaves, the lodge at Shō-fu-den fits into the category of peristyle bungalows. The former exhibition hall was divided into three parts: a sitting room at the southwest end; a central, high-ceilinged living room with fireplace inglenook and other recesses;

Fig. 133

and an equally tall dining room. The interior featured exposed wood framing, with gold-leafed and painted or stenciled panels, finely grilled fenestration covered with rice paper to soften the light, and bronze chandeliers and coffered ceilings overhead. Furniture was fashioned for the house in the contemporary, craftsman manner.

Fig. 37

The Canmack cottage in Tuxedo Park and Shō-fu-den were joined by two other Japanese-type complexes in the Catskills built within a few years of the latter. One was Grey Lodge, near Denning, the summer residence of Alexander Tison, who had taught law at the Imperial University in Tokyo from 1889 to 1894; and the other was Yama-no-uchi (Home in the Mountains), an exclusive caravanserai near Napanoch conducted by Mr. and Mrs. Frank Seman.[8]

Fig. 134

The Kinkaku was of importance equal to the Main Pavilion in the Imperial Japanese Garden at the Saint Louis exposition. Its encircling galleries on several levels was a familiar image, beginning with such a

Fig. 7

humble structure as Gandy's early-nineteenth-century dairy in England, including the raised-cottage type in the Deep South, memorialized at

Fig. 21

the Chicago fair in the Louisiana Building, and filtering down to the

Fig. 58

miniscule Blanche Sloan bungalow at Jamaica, Long Island, which (built a few years after the fair) may even have been inspired by the Kinkaku. The archetype of this building had been constructed in 1394 for the third Ashikaga shōgun, Yoshimitsu, as a semi-religious retirement home near Kyoto. After his death it was converted into a temple, Rokuanji, which included other buildings. Its name (the Golden Pavilion) derived

134. Kinkaku in the Imperial Japanese Garden at the Louisiana Purchase Exposition. *The International Studio*, May 1905.

from the upper part's being gilded; and many people consider it one of the world's most beautiful and perfect buildings. The Saint Louis version left something to be desired, and it was spoiled by gaudy striped awnings hanging from the eaves. Nevertheless, it attracted considerable attention.

One of its admirers was a steamboat pilot from New Orleans, Capt. M. Paul Doullut, who erected a home at the river end of Egania Street in 1905. In sympathy with his calling, the design combined Mississippi River packet elements with the Ashikaga silhouette. Galleries are both porches and decks, with railings and slender posts, between which an original touch is the wooden balls, graduated in size like a pearl necklace, strung on metal wires. The superstructure is equally cupola and pilothouse. Chimneys, proper to neither steamboat nor Japanese dwelling,

Fig. 135

THE AMERICAN BUNGALOW

135. Captain M. Paul Doullut House, New Orleans, La. Photo 1954.

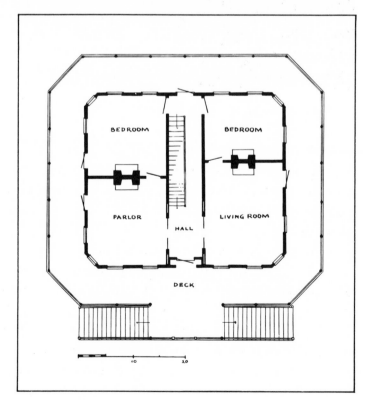

136. Upper or Main-floor Plan of the Doullut House. Measured and drawn by the author.

are reduced to brick stubs, out of which rise metal smoke funnels. Pressed steel crestings crown the cornices. Corners are chamfered, and there are elliptical windows containing stained-glass in the narrow angle planes. Doors either open out or slide back into wall pockets as in ships. The plan is nautical in having narrow corridors and steep gangway stairs. The front end of the upper hall has been converted into a bathroom, with a small window replacing the former recessed doorway. A replica of the Kinkaku-steamboat bungalow was built across the street for a son. The only voyage the pair ever made was when they were towed back from the river at the time the levee was extended along this stretch of the Mississippi River.

Fig. 136

Another Japanesque extravaganza was a vacation house on Lake Steilacoom in Washington State. It was planned by the Los Angeles architect I. Jay Knapp for Leo H. Long, and was described as "not a Shintō temple from the Island Empire of Japan, but an original idea for a Summer cottage among the pines. . . ."[9] Its reduplication of dipping gables might be compared to those of a fortified castle rather than a Shintō shrine. Their tin roofs curl up more than in any prototype. Ridge poles are given an open treatment quite "Queen Anne" in character,

Fig. 137

137. Leo H. Long Vacation House on Lake Steilacoom, Wash. I. Jay Knapp, Architect. *The Architect*, November 1915.

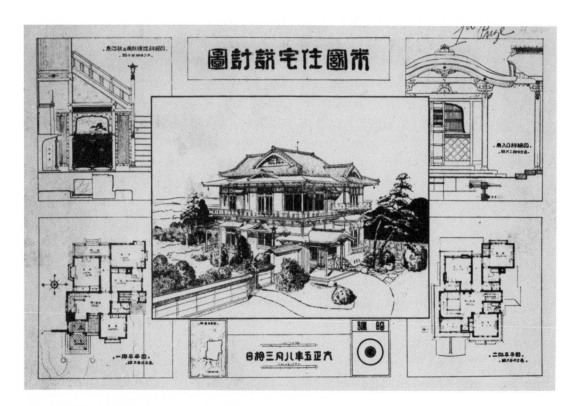

138. First Prize Design for a River View House by Iwao Shimizu.
Yamanaka Competition. *Architecture*, February 1917.

and diagonally crossed timbers, set on the apex to hold down thatching,
here are elevated, anticipating wireless antennas. The chimney bristles
with hornlike protruberances. A quaint paling of natural branches
excludes intruders from new planting in front of the veranda, and
matches the rustic armchair placed on the lawn in the foreground.

The peak of exotic high-style bungalows was reached in designs
responding to a competition sponsored by Yamanaka and Company,
importers of Eastern art objects to the United States since the early
1890s. The contest was open to young architects in Japan. Specifications
called for a suburban residence of two stories with garret and basement,
to contain living and dining rooms, library, kitchen, pantry, four bedrooms, and a bath, not to cost more than $20,000. Although it was to be
pure Japanese in dress, there were to be no *tatami*, or mats, on the
floors. The house was to be placed on a lot measuring 100 by 150 feet,
lying between a highway and a large river. Entries were to be submitted

SPECIALIZED TYPE BUNGALOWS **175**

139. The *Lexington Herald* Model Home in Lexington, Ky.
Frankel and Curtis, Architects. Photo by John C. Wyatt, 1974,
Courtesy of the *Lexington Herald-Leader*.

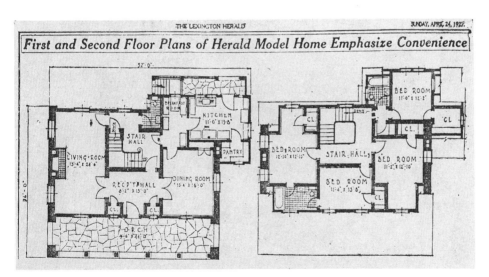

140. Floor Plans of the Model Home in Lexington.
Lexington Herald, 24 April 1927, Model Home Section.

in Japan by 31 August 1916, or would be accepted at the Yamanaka shop
on Fifth Avenue, New York, up to October 15th.

The first prize, accompanied by a purse of 300 yen, was awarded to
Iwao Shimizu of Tokyo. In this design the residence was situated about
halfway back and near the north boundary of the lot. The building was *Fig. 138*

THE AMERICAN BUNGALOW

141. Restored Perspective Sketch of the Samuel W. Cockrell House, Eutaw, Ala.

142. The Cockrell House Remodeled into a Bungalow. Photo 1977.

compact, yet pleasingly articulated into various pavilions, covered with convex tiled roofs, low concave pent roofs, and adorned with curvilinear gables, balconies, and porches. The plan was beautifully thought out, with entry to the side of the portico, library and lavatory opening off the front hall, and living and dining rooms at the rear, for enjoyment of the fine view. Kitchen and service stairs were reached by a side portal. In addition to the four chambers (one an enclosed sleeping porch) upstairs were two full baths, each with the water closet in a separate compartment. Unifying both stories was the stairway with its generous open well. Centrally heated, the interior bungalow feature missing is the fireplace, with an inglenook in the living room; in place of the latter is a *tokonoma*, or alcove for flower or art-object display. The third prize in the Yamanaka competition, bestowed upon Koichi Kuroda, Tokyo, resembled the Japanese dwelling at the Philadelphia Centennial.[10]

If exotic types lent themselves to the bungalow pattern, European colonial building in America did as well. Near the beginning of this chapter we saw the adaptation of Spanish colonial from the West; let us now turn full circle by looking at a bungalow inspired by Dutch colonial on the East Coast. The example was built in a new suburb in Lexington, Kentucky, across from Henry Clay's historic home, Ashland. A 75-foot-wide tract was purchased by the *Lexington-Herald* newspaper in August of 1926, and the local architectural firm of Frankel and Curtis was commissioned to design a model home. It had gabled end walls of stone, and the rest of the building was frame. An arch in either flank opened to a square-piered gallery across the front. Above it was placed a wide box dormer. The box dormer is an over-sized Dutch dormer, *Fig. 139* earlier seen on the Pitcher bungalow house in Maine. On the *Herald* *Fig. 49* house it gives something of the effect of a double-pitched or gambrel roof, as in the Lefferts house on Long Island. Roof overhangs on the *Fig. 18* gable ends and flagstones on the porch floors characterize the Lexington house as a bungalow. Also, the floor plans are complex, in large measure due to having to provide sufficient baths, closets, and kitchen annexes proper to a pre-Depression model home. It was decorated and *Fig. 140* furnished by twenty-six local firms and opened during Better Home week at the end of April, 1927. The house sold early the following month for $16,488.[11]

An old Greek Revival residence in Alabama had been remodeled into a form similar to that of the *Lexington-Herald* house at a prior date.

THE AMERICAN BUNGALOW

Fig. 141

Fig. 142

It was built in the middle of the nineteenth century for Samuel W. Cockrell on a 131-acre estate adjoining the town of Eutaw. The property was acquired by the West Alabama Real Estate Company in 1909, and the land was surveyed and laid out in lots by T. P. Kemp.[12] The driveway of the old Cockrell house was made the principal street of the new subdivision and called Eutaw Avenue. The residence was moved to one side, reoriented to face the street, and set closer to the ground. Chimneys were rebuilt in an irregular manner; the portico was replaced by a veranda spanning the facade and continuing to one side as a porte-cochere, and the box dormer was added. The final result reflected newly built bungalows in the neighborhood, only it was larger. Its roof was more steeply pitched and lacked overhanging raking eaves, and the remaining doorway and fenestration were of different character.

The specialized type bungalows examined vary considerably in style, stemming from Amerindian-Spanish, Hellenistic-Roman, American-pioneer, Scandinavian, Alpine, Japanese, Dutch, and Greek Revival antecedents. Besides period, their one common denominator is the generous roof, and some of them were favored by a hill or mountainous setting.

NOTES

1. W. H. Ansell, "An interesting Bungalow," *The Brickbuilder*, March 1908, p. 59.

2. Henry H. Saylor, *Bungalows*, Philadelphia, 1911, pp. 25, 28.

3. William Phillips Comstock, *Bungalow Camps and Mountain Homes*, New York, 1908, p. 103.

4. Interview with Mrs. Curtis Freshel before her death in 1948. Her residence, Providence House, may be seen to the left of the Norwegian house (fig. 127).

5. Such as Charles Alma Boyes, "The Swiss Chalet in American," *House and Garden*, August 1908, pp. 59–60; Louis J. Stellmann, "The Swiss Chalet Type for America," *ibid.*, November 1911, pp. 290–292.

6. Dr. Jokichi Takamine came to America in 1884 as a commissioner to the New Orleans World's Industrial and Cotton Centennial Exposition, and he returned in 1890 to apply in the distilling industry the starch-digesting enzyme *Takadiastase* that he had developed. In 1901 he isolated adrenalin from the suprarenal gland, which earned him an international reputation. He married an American.

7. An advertisement at the time of the sale of Shō-fu-den gives statistics and is illustrated with four photographs. *Country Life in America*, April 1916, p. 5.

8. Clay Lancaster, *Japanese Influence in America*, New York, 1963, pp. 144–154.

9. *The Architect*, November 1915, p. 245.

10. *Architecture*, February 1917, p. 34.

11. Deed Book 243, p. 175, Fayette County records. See Bettye Lee Mastin, "Local Firms Helped Herald Build House at 117 Sycamore in 1927," *Sunday Herald-Leader*, 20 October 1974, p. E-12.

12. Plat Deed Book 14, p. 83, Greene County records.

VII

THE BOX BUNGALOW

EXCESSIVE NATIONWIDE PATRONAGE for popular housing tended to strip the bungalow of style, or at least of historic architectural style. The bulk of the American public was interested primarily in homes providing a livable and what it considered a pleasant atmosphere, with more emphasis upon comfort than culture. Functionalism—meaning holding to stark essentials—was embraced only in the rarest instances, as the idea was ingrained that everything made had to be elaborated, that is, "prettied up." Those who designed and built for this community complied with its taste, and the result was an avalanche of bungalows constituting a realm unto themselves. They were specimens of detached minimal housing, a sort of family packaging, as it were, which might be referred to as box bungalows. Many were mass-produced, mail-order, ready-made homes that were conceived by a company employee, whose products went out to all parts of the country. All looking alike, they had not the slightest vestige of regional characteristics. But on the whole they held to the fundamental bungalow traits, such as low forms and snug plans, and the dominating roof. The restricted size of these essays often prompted artifices for superficial individualization, such as unnecessarily complex roof shapes (gable reduplication and elaborated dormers), the application of quasi-constructural decoration (to brackets, rafter ends, and bargeboards) and combining several materials to further complicate a normally simple member (such as porch posts). It is more noticeable in these plainer bungalows that the fenestration follows that of the early (1879) summer house at Monument Beach, many of the windows being wide (of two or three lights) and having upper sashes divided into small panes, and a single pane below. Consistent with the tendency to break up spaces at moderate cost was the use of the trellis. It served to screen the unsightly, such as the bare earth between piers under the front porch and household utensils accumulated on the back porch, and for a degree of privacy and shade to benefit relaxing householders around outdoor areas.

Fig. 44

The box bungalow, as a special phase, embraced the miniscule, fragile, and temporary manifestations. They related to the camping experience and vacation shelter, and to the newlyweds' first housekeeping establishment from which they expected to move on to more substantial quarters. The simplest statement was the tent bungalow, such as was to be found in the Bungalow Camp of Dr. Fillmore Moore at Eliot, Maine, at the turn of the century. The camp was a "short trolley ride from old Portsmouth, New Hampshire, along the Dover route, with the winding Piscataqua ever in view." Dr. Moore's campers were subjected to a regimen of living "as much as possible in the open air . . . [eating] the right food in the right way . . . [and working] always to some purpose, with an eye for simple beauty, and with plenty of time for play."[1] The bungalows they inhabited varied from 9-by-12 feet to 20-by-32 feet in size, and the only solid parts were their framework, flooring, and a batten door, the roof and sides being of stretched canvas. Upper sections of the wall could be propped open. Units were provided with normal furniture, including stuffed and bentwood chairs, chests of drawers, and metal beds draped in mosquito netting, and the campers brought and used their own trunks.

Fig. 143

Fig. 144

Henry Saylor recognized the type in his comprehensive book on *Bungalows* published in 1911. He noted that "Similar to these temporary shacks [on the East Coast] in purpose and general character are the

143. A Guest Tent House at Bungalow Camp, Eliot, Me.
Good Housekeeping, June 1907.

144. Interior of the Guest Tent House at Bungalow Camp.
Good Housekeeping, June 1907.

tent-houses of Southern California, where the side walls are made of canvas stretched on frames. These are usually hinged so that the whole building may be thoroughly and quickly ventilated. Needless to say, the tent-house makes an ideal outdoor sleeping-room when arranged for that purpose, but its application to homes intended for other than merely occasional use is necessarily limited."[2] Special attention was called to the hinged frames because of their greater rigidity over the camp variety. The California tent-houses are altogether more substantial. Saylor shows three examples: each has a shingled hipped roof, small porch, and from three to six canvas-stretched frames per side. The smallest contains "two rooms and a shower bath . . . the cost was about $300."[3] Its lower walls are covered with clapboards. Another has upright flush boards under the canvas frames, a vent cupola on the roof, and a square brick chimney. All three have a few glazed windows; those of *Fig. 145* the one illustrated flank the door opening onto the porch.

In bungalow-land, or California, harboring the broadest assortment bearing the name of bungalow, one came upon some odd examples. Thus Alice Chittenden, an Eastern girl, was struck by the application of the term to a converted trolley during a visit to East Oakland in 1901. The arrested vehicle stood on the spacious grounds of a residence

Fig. 146

perched on the estuary overlooking the bay, and it was neither a full-time nor a summer home but a luxurious little retreat. The front and rear windows, as well as the center one of five on each flank, had been removed, and all but two were replaced by wood panels. The double windows on each side were outfitted with striped awnings. The coach was furnished with a studio couch, easy chairs, a mahogany tea table, and shelves filled with knickknacks, and overhead was "cunningly added a dome of stained glass." Its effect was that of Queen Victoria's private railroad carriage. The back platform was enclosed, a "Bagdad portiere" hung over the door, and narrow bookshelves were inserted in the former window openings to either side. The space behind was transformed into a "complete buffet and wine closet," including a "silver champagne cooler and chafing-dish."[4] A Chinese servant was provided to pass "the viands." His other duties made use of "such housekeeping appurtenances as a miniature sweeper, dustpan, feather duster and whisk broom," whose presence served to bring the conversion down to earthly bungalow level.

Such horse-drawn cars had been withdrawn from the streets of San Francisco and sold upon the introduction of electric trolleys in the late 1890s. A good many were purchased by Jacob Heyman and placed on the beach at Ocean Side, where they were resold with a narrow strip of ground. Heyman retained six, which were incorporated in a two-storied masonry structure for his own use.[5] It is not known to have been referred to as a bungalow.

145. A Tent Bungalow in Southern California. From a photograph in Henry H. Saylor, *Bungalows*, Philadelphia, 1911. Sketched by the author.

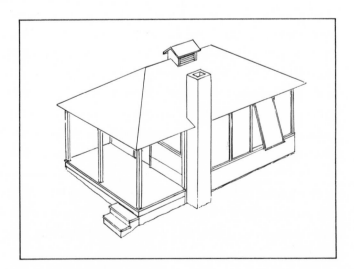

146. "A California Bungalow," Converted Trolley Car at East Oakland, Calif. *Good Housekeeping*, September 1901.

Returning from makeshift to constructed bungalows brings us to the minimum dwelling that was only a step removed from the tent-house. A representative design appeared in the July, 1909, issue of *Bungalow Magazine*. It is designated a "California Bungalow," and it reminds us of the primitive barn stage of the bungalow mentioned in Lazear's article on "The Evolution of the Bungalow" in *House Beautiful* (Chapter Five). The *Bungalow Magazine*'s version consists of an 18-by-28-foot vertical-plank shell covered by a low-pitched gable roof. It is only two-thirds the size of the largest tent dormitory at Bungalow Camp in Maine. The internal divisions are achieved by curtains suspended from poles supported by four posts and the outer walls. The middle portion is the living room with a corner fireplace in a chimneypiece that has the kitchen stove behind it. The sink is in the center recess at this end of the structure, the entrance vestibule at the front. Located opposite is the "living room alcove" with curtained spaces for beds front and back. A

Fig. 147

Fig. 148

147. A Small One-room California Bungalow of Vertical-plank Walls.
The Bungalow Magazine, July 1909.

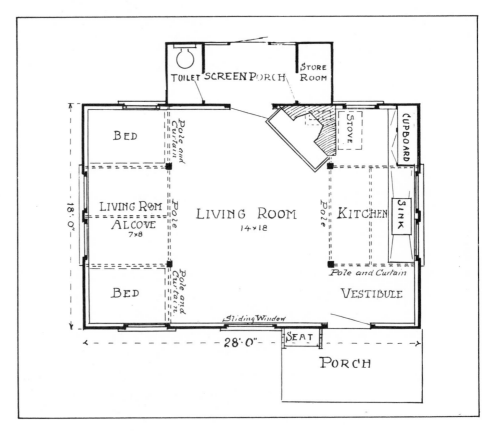

148. Plan of the One-room California Bungalow.
The Bungalow Magazine, July 1909.

screened porch appended to the rear interlays a store room and water closet. The kitchen sink doubles as lavatory. With curtains all around the interior effect is tentlike. Its flexibility relates to the Japanese house, with its sliding *fusuma*. The plainness of the house itself, recalling Dwyer's cabin or the simplest of Downing's examples, could have existed at this time had the bungalow never been heard of.

The wood alternative for exposed vertical plank walls was overlapping shingles, which West Coast architects often used on their more ambitious undertakings, and which could be used to dignify the small box bungalow. Peter B. Wight's discussion of "California Bungalows" in the October, 1918, issue of *The Western Architect* shows them covering little "Chinese Type" dwellings in Los Angeles and Hollywood. One in the latter's Formosa Court displays a naïve articulation of structural members about porches, outlandish upturned eaves, and trivial quaintness in masonry elements. The irregular brickwork of the chimney penetrates the roof overhang, as a stack, and becomes a projecting planter under the larger of the windows. Wight comments that whereas Charles

Fig. 149

149. "Chinese Type of Bungalow in Formosa Court, Hollywood."
The Western Architect, October 1918.

150. A "Chinese Pagoda [Grafted] on to the Not-Quite-Neo-Grecque" House. *Country Life in America*, 15 July 1912.

Sumner Greene had introduced "slight curvature . . . to all straight lines of roofs as refinement in design" the treatment here presents a poor effect at needless expense.[6] The house gives the impression of being a toy or a small trinket container with exaggerated elements so as not to escape attention. Such handling and its size keep the Formosa Court bungalow out of the architectural category (Chapter Six) and put it among the boxes.

In an article in the 15 July 1912 issue of *Country Life in America*, entitled "The Rampant Craze for the Bungle-oh," L. D. Thomson puns on the builder of such a structure by calling him a "bungler." One of a dozen examples illustrated is described as a "Chinese Pagoda [grafted] *Fig. 150* on to the Not-Quite-Neo-Grecque." Though having milder upturned eaves the prickliness of the roof of this larger exotic overshadows the Formosa Court bungalow. Either one is a far cry from the authentic Chinese house shown in the *American Architect*, accompanying Viollet-le-Duc's "Habitations," which would have been a credit to the Ameri- *Fig. 39* can bungalow movement. Comparison of the latest bungle with a pagoda is as remote as the Florida "Bungoda" mentioned in Chapter Three.[7]

As has been seen, references to far and former architectural styles were localized at the two outer shores of the American continent, whereas the prairie philosophy, of innate originality, predominated in the Central States. At Chicago, where the balloon frame originated early in the nineteenth century (Chapter Four), William A. Radford and several associates issued a book on *Practical Carpentry* in 1907. The following year, incorporated as The Radford Architectural Company, they launched *Radford's Combined House and Barn Plan Book*, with over 1,200 copper halftone plates, representing over 300 designs, and also *Radford's Artistic Bungalows*, a collection of 208 designs. In the introduction to the last, Radford declares: "The bungalow age is here. It is the renewal in artistic form of the primitive 'love in a cottage' sentiment that lives in some degree in every human heart. Architecturally, it is the result of the effort to bring about harmony between the house and its surroundings, to get as close as possible to nature. . . . It is 'homey,' and comes near to that ideal you have seen in the dreamy shadows of night when lying restless on your couch you yearned for a haven of rest." The bungalow's kinship to nature, by this time, has become a cliché no promoter would dare omit. But Radford's particular viewpoint is that of reverie and sentimentality, the dream cottage without anything so natural as roses covering it; in short, the valentine gift box of sweets presented and received in the parlor.

Out of consideration for what is expected by way of environment in the pictures of his bungalows, Radford sets them on a carpetlike lawn, traversed by runnerlike access walks, with an occasional petty urn holding an artificial-looking plant, and having a not-very-convincing arboreal backdrop. His bungalows are as though made of cardboard *Figs. 151,* stamped out by machinery. They are ornamented with stripes and lat- *152*

151. Perspective of Design No. 5031, *Radford's Artistic Bungalows*, Chicago, 1908.

152. Perspective of Design No. 5057, *Radford's Artistic Bungalows.*

tice patterns, flat dado panels, uniform windows that seem more for decorating the walls than for letting light in or visibility through, and they are crowned by lids rather then roofs. One expects that if the tops were laid back there would be revealed a family of dolls packed in excelsior inside. Both being practically square, having center recesses flanked by equal pavilions with triple windows, the two examples here shown in perspective suggest alternate external treatments for a single

Fig. 153   floor plan. But they are not. Design No. 5031 has a dining room running through the middle with inglenook at the end, a porch beyond, living room and kitchen on one side balancing two bedrooms on the other, with pantry between the former and the passage and bathroom between

Fig. 154   the latter. Design No. 5057 is entered by the insignificant door in the shorter side, leading into a vestibule and hall; the living room and dining room are right and left, and the remainder of the rooms can be reached only through the last. These include three bedrooms, bath, kitchen and pantry, and there is a back porch at the corner. As in a doll house, where the occupants are picked up and transferred from one room to another through the open ceiling or wall—shifted for momentary amusement—room uses and traffic patterns are not very well thought out. Radford furnished for his "artistic bungalows" blueprints of foundations and floor plans, front, rear, and side elevations, wall sections

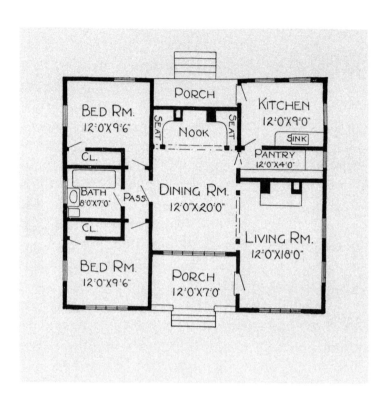

153. Floor Plan of Design No. 5031, *Radford's Artistic Bungalows*.

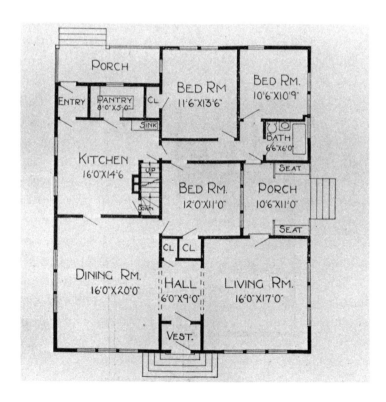

154. Floor Plan of Design No. 5057, *Radford's Artistic Bungalows*.

and "all necessary interior details." Accompanying specifications consisted of "twenty-two pages of typewritten matter." The cost was $10.

Entering the late bungalow period, when American creativity in domestic building was being channeled largely into foreign styles reminiscent of what had been seen by veterans returning from World War I, the bungalow generally settled down to being a prosaic commodity. It was readily obtainable as standard designs from plants convenient to expanding suburban sites. The 1925 catalog of the Lewis Manufacturing Company, Bay City, Michigan, offered ready-made parts for from four-room bungalows to twelve-room duplex houses. Also available were built-in features—buffets, bookcases, linen cases, room dividers, and breakfast nooks—porch and utility-room additions, disappearing stairs, and one- or two-car garages. One of the smaller bungalows was called *Fig. 155* "The Sylvan." It is nearly square and has a full-width front porch, and its hipped roof sports a dormer window. Porch supports are cobblestone piers capped by twin wood posts, with parapets matching the shingled walls. The plan is divided unequally front to back and bisected crosswise; the living room balances the kitchen and bath, and similar bedrooms *Fig. 156* are to the side. The arrangement would have been better if the kitchen exchanged places with the front bedroom, and both bedrooms opened from the hall accessible to the bath. The one tiny closet in the house would have made "The Sylvan" a likely candidate for a Lewis disappearing stairs to storage space in the garret, thus justifying its dormer window.

The Lewis Manufacturing Company called larger examples, with bedrooms on the second floor, "Semi-Bungalows." A design labeled "The *Fig. 157* Vallejo" had been built by a satisfied customer in Ohio. Its walls are shingled, and the ample front porch is covered by a lean-to roof. Massive supports are set between steps and corners, carrying low-arched beams. A gabled dormer is sufficiently large to house a nine-foot wide bedroom upstairs. The living room is made "particularly delightful" by "many windows, a fireplace, and semi-open stairs." Dining room, *Fig. 158* kitchen, pantry, and back porch complete the first-floor accommodations. Second-story bedrooms are small and of irregular shapes. Closets are under sloping roofs, and a bath is at the head of the stairs. Posts, doors, and brackets belonging to "The Vallejo" are recognized among parts *Fig. 159* ready for shipment in a photo at the back of the Lewis catalog.

Manufacturers picked up and modified each other's designs. Thus, six years later, the Gordon-Van Tine Company, Davenport, Iowa, in-

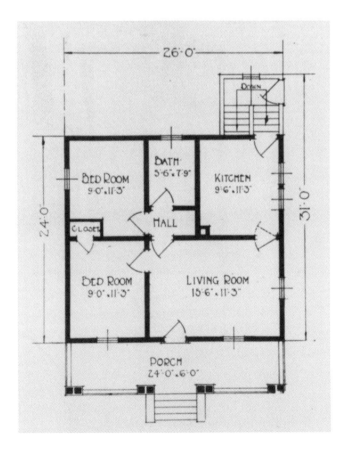

155. "The Sylvan," Bungalow in the Catalog of the Lewis Manufacturing Co., Bay City, Mich., 1925.

156. Floor Plan of "The Sylvan." Lewis Manufacturing Co. Catalog, 1925.

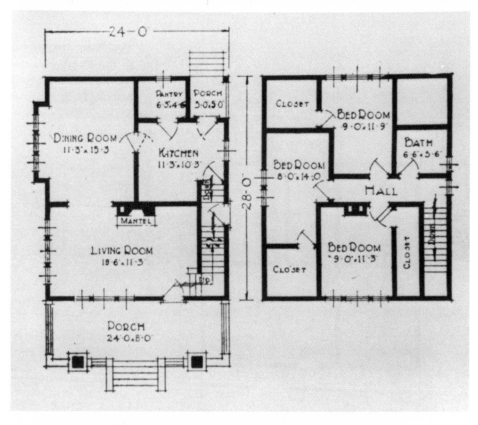

157, 158. "The Vallejo," Semi-Bungalow. Perspective Drawing and Floor Plan. Lewis Manufacturing Co. Catalog, 1925.

159. Assembled House Parts at the Lewis Manufacturing Co. Plant. Catalog, 1925.

cluded a reasonable facsimile of "The Vallejo" and called it "The Culver." It is four-feet wider and eight-feet deeper. The front door is centered, the living room smaller and without fireplace, and there are two bedrooms and bath on the first floor, with only two other bedrooms and a sewing room (in the front dormer) upstairs. The increase in magnitude takes "The Culver" out of the box category—but only because of its size. *Fig. 160*

The Gordon-Van Tine Company had been furnishing house parts since it was begun by Uriah N. Roberts in 1865. Horace G. Roberts was president in 1931, when "The Culver" was listed. The catalog's some seventy houses included thirty bungalows, the balance being divided among Colonial Revival houses, a sort of styleless block house, and a few Monterey Spanish and European designs. The numerical proportion indicated that the bungalow was on its way out. Still, there were versions possessing some charm. "The Redwood" is basically rectangular, but the dining room projects beyond its right flank, and it and the front porch are accented by extra bracketed gables with cutout terminals to the bargeboards. Walls are embellished with alternating long *Fig. 161*

160. "The Culver," Plan-cut House in the Catalog of the
Gordon-Van Tine Co., Davenport, Iowa, 1931.

Fig. 162

and narrow shingle courses, and a second material is introduced in brick piers, pedestals, antapodia, and chimney. The upper part of the porch posts have tapered wood shafts, and base and capital moldings. Boards and banisters combine for interest in the porch and terrace railings. A small library adjoins the living room, and, as in so many bungalows, the hall accessible to bedrooms and bath can be reached only through the dining room. However, one bedroom opens directly from the living room. The house is well supplied with closets, there being three for clothes, one for linen, and one for brooms. The sink is built into a counter that spans the entire outer wall of the kitchen. The Gordon-Van Tine Company encouraged customers' variations and furnished altered materials accordingly. It also accepted sketches and had its design department develop drawings, specifications, and estimates, which were submitted to the home builder for his approval or further changes. The aim to please stepped up the sale of materials, though it did little to improve the quality or sensitivity of the design.

The mail-order business lacked the individually concerned architect, who molded the house to the site and to the conditions that it was meant to serve into a unified whole. The sequence of the draftsman grinding out drawings, the mill cutting them out, and the local builder

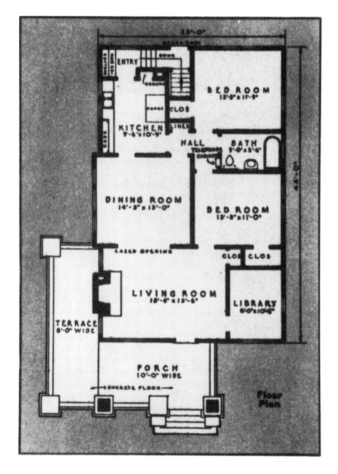

161. "The Redwood,"
Bungalow, Gordon-Van Tine Co.
Catalog, 1931.

162. Floor Plan of "The
Redwood." Gordon-Van Tine Co.
Catalog, 1931.

assembling them was a deadly process. Nothing distinctive could be had. As Charles Sumner Greene observed, architecture is not a predetermined commodity. It does not stem from patterns nor come out of a computer. He used the metaphor of the ready-made suit: it "will cover any man's back but a gentleman's."[8] Personal attention must focus on the unique product from first to last. The true bungalow is the exact antithesis of the mass-produced box bungalow. The box bungalow ignored the ideals for which the bungalow stood. It was an economic expedient; it served material and materialistic ends. The box bungalow lowered the standards to such a degree as to drain the movement of vitality. In this box the American bungalow was embalmed and buried.

NOTES

1. "A Bungalow Camp," *Good Housekeeping*, June 1901, p. 653.

2. Henry H. Saylor, *Bungalows, Their Design, Construction and Furnishing, with Suggestions Also for Camps, Summer Houses and Cottages of Similar Character*, Philadelphia, 1911, pp. 31, 33.

3. *Ibid.*, p. 38.

4. Alice Chittenden, "A California Bungalow," *Good Housekeeping*, September 1901, pp. 195–198.

5. *Country Life in America*, March 1907, p. 492.

6. Peter B. Wight, "California Bungalows," *The Western Architect*, October 1918, p. 99.

7. Thomson's article is sound in belittling quaintness in bungalows, but he makes the error of condemning motifs and materials. Stripes and plaids, one concedes, can be overdone in bungalow designing, and so can the use of cobblestones (as in the "peanut brittle" style). But he pictures the Irwin house (viewed from North Grand Avenue) to illustrate the last point, and certainly one would look far to find a better and more appropriate application of this native substance in creating a pleasing architectural effect than here.

8. Charles Sumner Greene, "Impressions of Some Bungalows and Gardens," *The Architect*, December 1915, p. 252.

VIII

BUNGALOW PLANS, INTERIORS, AND FURNISHINGS

BUNGALOWS VARIED INSIDE as greatly as in their outer forms, which takes into consideration the arrangement of rooms, circulation, flow of space, style and interior treatment, and built-in and movable furniture. The layout derived as much from the architectural environment out of which it grew as had the form, and we might start looking for its roots in the first houses built in North America. Chapter Two touched on the various nations that shared in the settling of this country, and of their contributions to its building tradition. Inasmuch as the bungalow eschewed architectural frills—theoretically—and harked back to the basic shelter, let us begin at this point.

Early English colonists, whether in Virginia, Massachusetts, Pennsylvania, or elsewhere along the Atlantic seaboard, built a remarkably similar first permanent home. It was two-storied; if one room per floor, it measured about 20-by-30 feet in plan, and if doubled, its length was about 40 feet. In Virginia and New England the stairway usually ascended from a "porch," or a vestibule that opened to the outside as well as to the main room(s); whereas in the Middle Colonies the stairs more commonly were accessible only to the rooms. In either case the stairway adjoined the chimney, both in the single and double house. Foundation remains of one unit of the brick Country House (1662–66) at Jamestown, and a restoration of the frame Jethro Coffin house (1686) on Nantucket illustrate the point. Perhaps in the Virginia example and certainly in the Massachusetts house the rear portion was a later addition. In another type of development the stairway was separated from the chimney. In the Arthur Allen house (before 1655) in Surrey County, Virginia, the staircase was in an appendage centered on the rear, balancing the porch pavilion on the front. In the stone Henry Whitfield house (1639–40) at Guilford, Connecticut, there was a square stair tower in the angle of the L-shaped building. From these basic types evolved a great assortment of combined elements. They became the bungalow's first native plan sources.

Fig. 163

The classic phase of American architecture (late Colonial and Federal periods) linked the adoption of the orders with symmetrical room dispo-

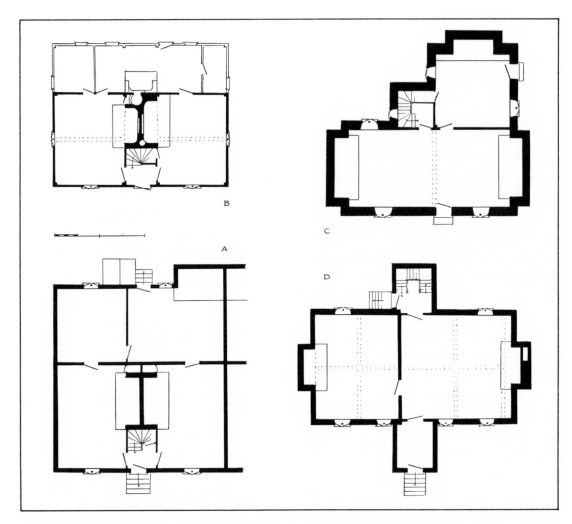

163. First-floor Plans of: A—One Unit of the Country House, Jamestown, Va.; B—Jethro Coffin House, Nantucket, Mass.; C—Henry Whitfield House, Guilford, Conn.; D—Arthur Allen House, Surry County, Va. All are seventeenth century. Drawn by the author.

sition to either side of a center hall, which was taken so much for granted that few plans appeared in the builder's guides. However, interior diversity was achieved by the introduction of rooms of odd shapes, such as the elliptical rooms in James Hoban's White House (1792), circular rooms in Dr. William Thornton's The Octagon (1798–1800), both in Washington, and octagons in Thomas Jefferson's Monticello (after 1796) and Poplar Forest (1806–09) in Albemarle and Bedford counties, Virginia. The Greek Revival did not as readily endorse the polygon, but it nevertheless abounded in spatial effects gained by recesses, screens of columns replacing walls, and the use of large mirrors multiplying room images. The finest achievement in this regard is Gaineswood (begun 1842), after designs by its owner, General Nathan Bryan Whitfield, at Demopolis, Alabama.[1]

We have seen that emphasis on interior arrangement was a trait of house-plan books beginning in the 1840s. In Downing, even cottages that were symmetrical outside were given room variety. Interior complexity was assured with the introduction of casual massing; it was a return to the character established in the early Henry Whitfield house in Connecticut. In Downing's Swiss cottage, although all rooms are rectangular (for the sake of structural economy), no two are the same size, same shape, or on axis with one another. It was such a plan that the bungalow adopted thirty to fifty years later. The Pitcher bungalow at Grindstone Neck introduced (to the bungalow province) the juxtaposition of wings at an obtuse angle. It led to the change of direction that became the dominant theme in the Pratt residence in the Ojai.

Figs. 27,
29, 30

Fig. 31

Figs. 44, 47,
51, 129

Fig. 96

The earliest California bungalows showed little plan indebtedness to the East Coast school, despite the fact that the Greene brothers had apprenticed to several Boston architectural firms before leaving for the West Coast.[2] The Bandini-bungalow group, having narrow wings at right angles embracing a court, was a railroad-car arrangement, entered one through another, or from the gallery serving as a corridor.

Fig. 80

The Greenes' complex houses present a different story. Part of the intricacy of the Irwin bungalow stems from its being a reworking of an earlier house. There are plan affinities with the center-garden house at Winters; but whereas all of the rooms in the Winters house are adjacent to the open court, at least seven rooms in the Pasadena residence are not.

Fig. 88
Fig. 76

There are differences between the Blacker house and its prototype plan by Hunt and Grey. The masonry example is as much separated part from part inside as outside. The Greene brothers' frame house shows considerably more spaciousness and flexibility; the recessed porch has been eliminated in favor of a larger hall, openings from it to the living and dining rooms have been expanded, doors and windows have been made triple or multiple, and the wall dividing dining room from the glass porch can be entirely folded back. The parapeted flat terrace of the Hunt and Grey scheme has been replaced by strips of paving, with steps at intervals, that cling to the building and follow the contours

Figs. 89, 90

164. Dining Room of the Charles
M. Pratt House, Nordhoff, Calif.
Greene and Greene, Architects.
Photo by Marvin Rand.

of the site, tying the two together, at one end entering the pergola that
forms an extension to the dining-room wing. One can go no further in
linking limited inner volume with unlimited outer space.

Parallels between the Pratt bungalow and a summer cottage by
Katherine C. Budd have been noted in terms of shape and disposition
of rooms (Chapter Five). It further might be pointed out here that the
Figs. 95, 96 bungalow surpasses the cottage in achieving an interior space flow. The
center wedge, or living hall, at Nordhoff, has been lengthened, and the
porch side is dissolved into three sets of glazed double doors. Opposite,
triple glass doors, with paired windows to either side, open onto the
front terrace. The spreading volume of this living hall of modest height
Fig. 164 lifts to the tall square dining room adjoining. The space is further
regulated by built-in furniture in corners and recesses, such as the seats
and sideboard. The interior finish of the house is entirely of wood, with
exposed beams to flat ceilings downstairs, and trusses to the sloping
ceilings of the second story.

The core of the bungalow is the living room, its presence being one of the bungalow's distinguishing characteristics. Although room uses on the plan of the vacation house at Monument Beach are not identified, it is apparent that the one with the fireplace and bay window is the living room. In the Brunner bungalow the "hall" is too axial to be a parlor and therefore serves as a living room. Beginning with the Pitcher house, the living room is labeled (marked "L. R."), and the practice continues uninterruptedly. Let us look into the genesis of this phenomenon called the living room. It is equivalent to the "hall" in the seventeenth-century house. Downing used the term initially in two "Toll-gate House" designs in the 1847 edition of *Cottage Residences*.[3] One is of a low building of three rooms (including a kitchen and bedroom). The second is two-storied and adapted from an inn published in John Loudon's *Supplement*. Downing's has a parlor, and the living room is where meals are served. Instances in which the term appears in *Downing's Country Houses* (1850) apply to rooms accompanied by a parlor, and all were used for dining. By the last quarter of the nineteenth century the living room had been freed from eating purposes and there was a legitimate dining room. The living room was quite different from the old-fashioned parlor, which "was opened on Sundays, on Thanksgiving-day, for funerals, for weddings, and on the one or two occasions in the year when the awful solemnity of a formal 'party' was gone through."[4] The living room is informal, and its first requisite is that its furniture be comfortable (Wakefield contour, rattan pieces, Chinese bamboo reclining chairs, lounges, sofas, and stools, and multi-use furniture were recommended); and the second is that it "admit the ornaments of life—casts, pictures, engravings, bronzes, books, chief nourishers in life's feast; but in the beginning these are to be few."[5] Written on the eve of the bungalow's debut, the statements quoted reflected the advanced thinking of the times and anticipated the upcoming trend.

The focus of the living room is the fireplace. A unique bungalow treatment was its incorporation in and elaboration as an inglenook. Inglenooks feature in floor plans of the Alvord house in Brooklyn and in a mountain retreat, the latter accompanied by a perspective drawing, and one appears in the interior photograph of the Gamble house. More attention was directed toward the fireplace by the inglenook enframement than by any other means. The cozy recess in front of the fire, usually flanked by seats, probably came into existence in medieval

Fig. 44
Fig. 47
Fig. 49

Figs. 29, 30, 31

Figs. 59, 118
Fig. 94

houses having tremendous fireplaces, which were closed up in favor of a smaller hearth, and the former chimney area was converted into the inglenook. It was the corner made famous by little Jack Horner's discovery of the plum, where one could sit in comfort out of the drafts that blew around the great hall. The inglenook was resurrected in England during the late Gothic Revival period, as in the Vallance house (1867–69)

Fig. 165

at Farnham Royal, Buckinghamshire. The feature was adopted by the "Queen Anne" style, and accompanied it to the United States. Several are included in William W. Woolley's *Old Homes Made New*, published in New York in 1878, a collection of sketches and plans showing how to modernize stock period houses. Innovations included icing them with gables, eaves, fancy chimneys, towers, bay windows, gingerbread verandas, and equally ornate elements within—including inglenooks. Plate 16 depicts an example resembling that in the Vallance house of a decade earlier, except that the American is enframed by a segmental arch.

Fig. 15

The inglenook appeared in early English bungalows. In the United States it figured in smaller no less than in larger bungalows. Four out of the eleven six-room units in Saint Francis Court, Pasadena, had fireplace inglenooks (Nos. 1, 2, 9, and 11), and one other (No. 3) had a recessed

Fig. 114

fireplace. A typical living room in this group had light-colored plastered

165. Inglenook in the H. Vallance House, Farnham Royal, Bucks, England. W. E. Nesfield, Architect. C. L. Eastlake, *A History of the Gothic Revival*, London, 1872.

166. Living Room in No. 1 Saint Francis Court, Pasadena, Calif.
Sylvanus Marston, Architect. H. H. Saylor, *Bungalows*, Philadelphia, 1911.

walls, natural wood trim, and matching craftsman furniture, including
that built into the inglenook. American examples, as here, mostly are
arch-enclosed.

Fig. 166

Craftsman furniture fitted hand in glove with the American bungalow.
The beginnings of the former also can be traced back to mid-nineteenth-
century England, in a movement connected with the Domestic Revival
in architecture (Chapter One). Its progenitors were William Morris and
Philip Webb, later followed by Bruce Talbert, Edwin W. Godwin, Charles
L. Eastlake, C. F. A. Voysey, A. H. Mackmurdo, and L. R. Ashbee. Generally known on its home ground as the Arts and Crafts Movement, its
early affiliation was with the medieval, and in its late phase with the
highly styled Art Nouveau, as in the work of M. H. Bailie Scott.[6] The
taste of one of these men, Charles L. Eastlake, was set forth in his
designs shown in *Hints on Household Taste*, published at London in
1868. Nowhere in this volume is an entire room pictured, only pieces of
furniture, whose articulation into panels, turned and (often preciously)
decorated members established a style bearing his name. Although by
Nesfield, the inglenook at Farnham Royal, reproduced in Eastlake's later
book, *A History of the Gothic Revival*, is in his manner. Such designs

Fig. 165

were as much at home in "Queen Anne" buildings of the 1870s to '90s as craftsman-mission was to be in the American bungalow a generation later.

The Arts and Crafts Movement in England stimulated a response in America, prompting such books as George Ward Nichols's *Art Education Applied to Industry*, New York, 1877, and Arthur MacArthur's *Education in Its Relation to Manual Industry*, New York, 1884. These in turn gave rise to the manual training program in schools, such as that attended by the Greene brothers in Saint Louis. "Craftsman" is simply a more professional-sounding name than "manual training," but they mean the same thing. Both imply the actual making of an individualized piece. Charles Sumner Greene applied it to the architecture of bungalows, as stated in the last paragraph of the preceding chapter.

One of the most accomplished leaders of the American craftsman school primarily was concerned with graphic arts. He was Will H. Bradley, reputed to have been the highest paid commercial artist of the pre-World War I period in the United States.[7] His pictorial work was in the Art Nouveau manner, having the crispness of Aubrey Beardsley's drawings, and he turned out posters, advertisements, and illustrations for such magazines as *Harper's Bazaar* and for books, and he perhaps performed his best work in the printing-format field for the American Type-founders Company. Interior and furniture designs by him were in what has been called the mission style, a misnomer inasmuch as the builders of early Franciscan missions in the Southwest and California developed no style of furniture, much less this one. By mission is meant a type in which the plank is very much in evidence, the furniture sometimes descending to the depth of being practically unregenerated lumber. The craftsman element postulated exposed joinery, with prominent mortise-and-tenon penetrations locked by pegs. Will Bradley was assigned the creation of a set of eight rooms for a hypothetical house, which was published in consecutive numbers of *The Ladies' Home Journal* during 1901–02. The second in the series, the library, "the keynote of the house," is typical of his designs, though somewhat on the heavy-handed side. The space is handled cubistically, as a volume of varying heights and setbacks, modified by slabs and blocks projecting

Fig. 167   into it. Structure is apparent, whether in ceiling beams or furniture members. The designer's first loves provide accents: decorative lettering and stylized designs on horizontals and in rug and cushion patterns, and there are framed pictures specially planned for specific spots. Fire-

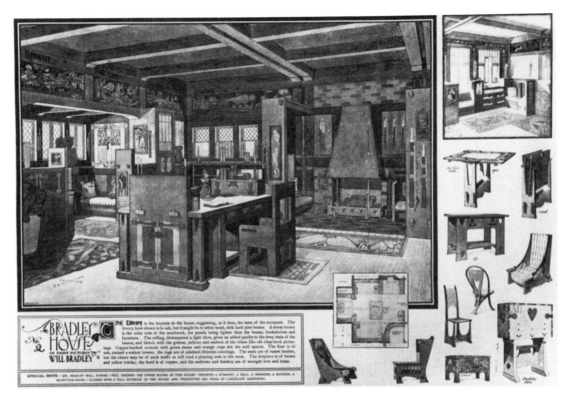

167. Design for a Library by Will H. Bradley. *Ladies' Home Journal*, December 1901.

place inglenook, window alcove, and built-in furniture fit the room into the bungalow category. As seen in margin designs, some of Bradley's furniture was given subtle curves reminiscent of Art Nouveau's whip-lash line, and he was fond of the heart shape.

Gustav Stickley was first and foremost a builder of furniture. He apprenticed to a manufacturer in his mid 'teens, and before he was thirty was in partnership with his two brothers making chairs. Later, Gustav and his brothers went their separate ways. During the early 1890s Gustav established the Stickley and Simons Company in Syracuse, New York. It initially made Eclectic furniture and reproductions of earlier styles. By the first of the new century he had turned to the craftsman type, and beginning in 1901 expanded his influence by editing and publishing a monthly magazine called *The Craftsman*; it continued through 183 issues over the next sixteen years. In 1908 he moved to Morris Plains, New Jersey, built a log bungalow, and established Crafts-

THE AMERICAN BUNGALOW

168. Settle, Sideboard and Two Arm Chairs Sketched from Stickley's 1909 Craftsman Furniture Catalog. Drawn by the author.

169. Rustic Swing Seat
and a Bed. Gustav
Stickley, *Craftsman Homes*,
New York, 1909.

man Farms. In 1913 he built the twelve-storied Craftsman Building
between East 38th and 39th streets in New York City. It housed offices
for his publication, show rooms for his furniture, a library, lecture hall,
restaurant, club rooms, and the Craftsman Permanent Homebuilders'
Exposition, containing spaces rented to manufacturers of building
materials, house and garden-grounds equipment, and interior-decora-
tion items. Unfortunately, Stickley over-extended himself; the entire
organization collapsed in 1916. At the peak of his career Stickley turned
out furniture largely of craftsman-mission design. Most was made of
native white oak, but some of it was of elm, chestnut, maple, and
beech; and there was leather, canvas or velour upholstery, with brass
studs and metal handles and hinges. Occasional chairs, armchairs,
rockers, settles, tables, desks, beds, cabinets, and sideboards were
among the offerings. The range of designs that Stickley's publications   *Fig. 168*
recommended for home craftsmen to make was wider, with rustic indoor

170. Designs for Two Hall Clocks. Stickley, *Craftsman Homes*.

Figs. 169, 170

and outdoor furniture at one extremity and neatly finished clock cases to accommodate purchased works at the other. Stickley did not foster too much competition by providing plans. The products manufactured at the Syracuse plant other than in the wood craftsman-mission line extended from Chinese Chippendale copies to willow chairs in furniture, and from table scarfs to wrought-iron andirons and hammered copper lighting fixtures in accessories.

Rooms in craftsman houses often featured unit planning and built-in furniture. A living room, first appearing in *The Craftsman* in 1905, has a fireplace recess deeper than the inglenook in the Saint Francis Court house: its ceiling is lower than the room's but not arched; the benches are lighter, somewhat Art Nouveau in style; and the mantel shelf carries

171. ''A Recessed Fireplace Nook in a Room where the Woodwork Is Light.'' Stickley, *Craftsman Homes*.

172. A Fireplace Corner in the Living Room to ''Cement Cottage No. 118.'' Gustav Stickley, *More Craftsman Homes*, New York, 1912.

across the seat backs. Wall panels in the recess and room proper are recommended to be covered with ''some fabric, such as silk, canvas, or Japanese grass cloth.'' Stickley liked doors with small glass panes in the upper part. A ''dropped ceiling'' is achieved by a plain upper section of the wall separated by a molding level with alcove and door height. A

Fig. 171

willow chair and craftsman plant stand with shelves are the only pieces of movable furniture shown.

A cozy retreat is found in the corner of another living room, focused on a hooded fireplace raised off the floor and framed in square tiles, which are similar to those that pave a sizable area in front. A bench to *Fig. 172* one side backs up to a wood screen behind which the staircase rises. The proximity of chimney and stairway is similar to that in the two seventeenth-century American houses shown at the first of this chapter, only here better related visually. The living room and dining room wrap around this central feature in a little cement cottage of six rooms and bath (the bedrooms and bath are upstairs) and the kitchen is tucked *Fig. 173* away back of the chimney. Fenestration is generous and some of it is

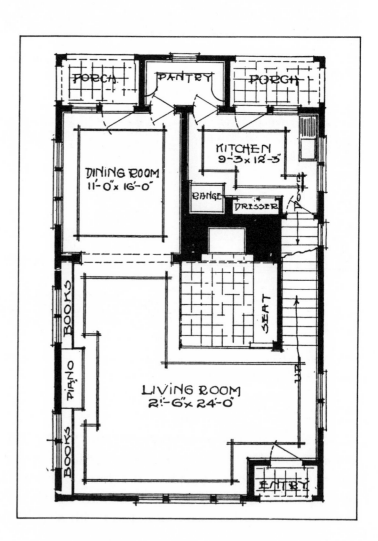

173. First-floor Plan of "Cement Cottage No. 118." Stickley, *More Craftsman Homes*.

174. Dining Room in the David B. Gamble Bungalow, Pasadena, Calif. Greene and Greene Architects. Photo 1954.

combined with door openings, filling the house with light, throwing emphasis upon the fireplace nook withdrawn into the shadows.

Frank Lloyd Wright used mission furniture in his early twentieth-century houses, some of it from his own designs. That for the B. Harley Bradley house (1900) in Kankakee bears the label of Leopold and J. George Stickley—Gustav's brothers—made at Fayetteville in New York. One can see the type in the cross-section of his *Ladies' Home Journal* house of 1901.

Fig. 71

The prime bungalow builders to create their own furnishings were Charles Sumner and Henry Mather Greene. They exerted complete control over their buildings, their settings, and their interiors. Furniture was made by Peter Hall after their specifications, and the brothers often took a hand in finishing pieces. Their furniture, while departing from historic models, avoids the mission look, being considerably more graceful. It is lighter in weight; its members have little affinity to the

Figs. 94,
174

THE AMERICAN BUNGALOW

175. A Corner of John Scott Bradstreet's Office in The Craftshouse, Minneapolis, Minn. *The House Beautiful*, June 1907.

plank but assume organic shapes. The construction, if less obvious than that of mission, is nevertheless apparent. In the base of the dining-room table in the Gamble house, for instance, the tenoned stretchers joining posts are pegged, and in such a way as to become a decorative element. The stepped-back uprights reflect the handrails of the stair-case in this house. Furniture in both the Gamble and Pratt houses (at least) display the cipher of Charles Sumner Greene. Colored glass in windows, doors, and lanterns was crafted by Emile Lange, who formerly had worked for Louis Comfort Tiffany, and who got his business on a paying basis—as had Peter Hall—largely through Greene and Greene patronage. Ceramics were executed by Gladding and McBean of Los Angeles. Rugs for the Gamble house were woven after the architects' designs in China.[8] Though considerably limited in area, as compared to the wide distribution and numerous makers of the mission, the Greene brothers' furniture surmounts mission as an aesthetic tour de force.

Another pocket of the craftsman domain was the Bradstreet Craft-house in Minneapolis, Minnesota. Its founder, John Scott Bradstreet, began his career with the Gorham Manufacturing Company of Providence, Rhode Island, and in 1874 he migrated to Minneapolis, where he set about introducing culture to this midwest community. He became the first president of its Art Institute in 1883. Several years later he opened the Crafthouse, and around 1900 remodeled an existing Italianate villa into its permanent headquarters. As in the Stickley building, a fair share of the Bradstreet establishment was an emporium, where furniture, art objects, and bric-a-brac, much of it imported, were sold. Bradstreet interiors were installed from coast to coast and up into Canada. The director's office was representative of the Crafthouse manner: Japanese influence is shown in the use of natural (often imported) woods, leather, metal, and sometimes tile, as is the panel treatment, the latter of which is also a bungalow characteristic, and the lattice casements of a bay window placed high off the floor is unreservedly so. American antiques were included in certain projects; the *Fig. 175* Federal and Empire pieces in the office, however, were from the old Bradstreet home in Massachusetts.

Lastly, in considering the bungalow interior, we come to the rooms of convenience, bathrooms and kitchens. Normally the bungalow, though containing up to four or five bedrooms, had only one bathroom. It measured 5-by-7 feet in size and held three fixtures, the lavatory, tub, and water closet. They were of white vitreous-finished cast iron or of

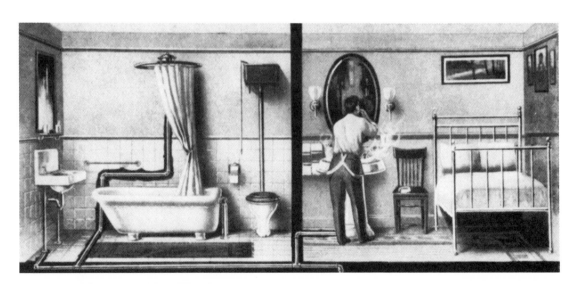

176. A Bathroom and Pedestal Lavatory in a Bedroom, from an Advertisement Issued by the Humphrey Co., Kalamazoo, Mich., a Manufacturer of Hot-water Heaters. Henry Collins Brown, *Book of Home Building and Decoration*, Garden City, N.Y., 1912.

ceramic, and often there was tile on the floor and partway up the walls. The basin might be set on a pedestal and the tub on feet or a solid base, and the water-closet tank was hung on the wall above head height, with pull chain for flushing, until after World War I, when the tank was lowered to present level. To relieve congestion, the water closet might

177. A "Well-Equipped Kitchen," Corner with Range and Work Table. Stickley, *Craftsman Homes.*

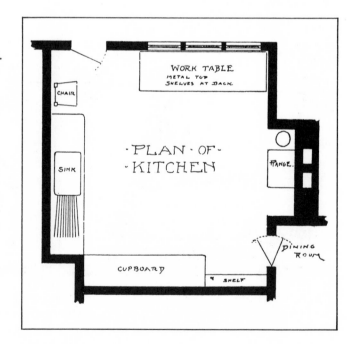

178. Plan of the "Well-Equipped Kitchen." Stickley, *Craftsman Homes.*

179. Corner of the "Well-Equipped Kitchen" with Built-in Cupboard and Sink. Stickley, *Craftsman Homes.*

be accommodated in a separate compartment, as in the Bandini bungalow, or an extra lavatory might be provided in the main bedroom.

Kitchens—as in the eleven units of Saint Francis Court—averaged 8-
by-12 feet. The sink and range or cooking stove were necessities, and
there would be a table and cupboards, but in no such proportion as one
finds today. "A Convenient and Well-Equipped Kitchen," which had
been in *The Craftsman* during 1905, shows a coal-burning range in a
recess that is shared with a gas hot-water heater, both ventilated to the
chimney behind. The metal-topped work table stands under a window
of three lights, with narrow shelves between for seasonings and other
food-preparation items and utensils. Drawers for accessories are imme-
diately below, and bins for flour and sugar are flanked by storage spaces
with hinged doors. Skillets and saucepans hang on a row of hooks at
the top of a tilelike wainscot, which the text says is of cement, as is the
floor. The sink is opposite, with a draining board on one side and
preparation shelf on the other, with pots and jugs suspended below,
and washing and drying objects hung on the wall. The accompanying
article recommends: "Ample cupboard space for all china should be
provided near the sink to do away with unnecessary handling and the
same cupboard, which should be an actual structural feature of the
kitchen, should contain drawers for table linen, cutlery and small

Fig. 80
Fig. 176

Fig. 177

Fig. 178

Fig. 179

utensils, as well as a broad shelf which provides a convenient place for serving." Missed in this plan is the ice box or refrigerator. It usually stood in an entry or on the back porch, and an 8-inch square card, numbered "25," "50," "75," and "100" was placed in a window (proper number up) to inform the ice man the poundage of the block needed.

The American bungalow possessed a well-integrated outer and inner personality. Its casualness was nowhere better expressed than in its living room. Even houses of the period with no external bungalow characteristics—like Colonial Revival, Norman, and Elizabethan—embraced the bungalow living room inside. It was open to everybody. Whereas small children had been banned from the old parlor, with its fragile chairs and vulnerable displays on the what-not, the furnishings of the bungalow living room were sufficiently rugged to withstand reasonable abuse, and welcomed them. Natural wood does not depreciate from the chips and scratches that disfigure painted, veneered, and gilded pieces. This naturalness set the pace for a household without complexes. It provided a constant reminder of the importance of shunning false surfaces. All of the life and of the parts of the bungalow revolved around the living room. It kept them in good order. Never had the small house been so well zoned. It was its concentration upon a vital, ample family center that made the bungalow great, its exposure of basic materials in their native colors that made it appealing, and its contents of convenient and comfortable furnishings that made it home.

NOTES

1. "The Story of Gaineswood," *House and Garden*, November 1939, pp. 41–44, 66; Clay Lancaster, *Greek Revival in Alabama*, Alabama Historical Commission, Montgomery, 1976, figs. 23–26, 38A–38B.

2. Charles S. Greene worked for H. Langford Warren, and Winslow and Wetherell; Henry M. Greene was with Shepley, Rutan and Coolidge, and Chamberlin and Austin.

3. A. J. Downing, *Cottage Residences*, New York, 1847, pp. 171–173.

4. Clarence Cook, *The House Beautiful*, New York, 1877, Chapter II, "The Living Room" (pp. 46–195), p. 47.

5. *Ibid.*, p. 84. Description of the "Oriental . . . combination of luxury . . . chair," p. 154.

6. Helena Hayward, ed., *World Furniture*, New York, 1965, pp. 220–[231].

7. Robert Koch, "Will Bradley," *Art in America*, 1962, p. 82.

8. Clay Lancaster, "My Interviews with Greene and Greene," *Journal of the American Institute of Architects*, July 1957, pp. 202–206. See also: Randell L. Makinson, *Greene & Greene: Furniture and Related Designs*, Santa Barbara and Salt Lake City, 1979.

IX

BUNGALOW SITE PLANNING AND GARDENING

THE FIRST HOUSES called bungalows in the United States were adjusted to their setting, rather than having their setting adjusted to them. Being summer cottages, on the water, their site was usually rocky, sandy, and supported little vegetation; and because they existed for vacation relaxation, there was little or no incentive to go against this propriety by gardening. Besides, planting is a spring and autumn occupation, when nobody was around to attend to it. The bungalows at Monument Beach, Grindstone Neck, Onawa, and Robbins Point, therefore, when occupied, looked as though their tenants had just arrived. With the bungalow at Newton Centre the situation was the reverse: it was occupied year-round, and its environs were different and treated in the Downingesque manner. A few shrubs were against the house, and a natural clump served for foreground interest. The two bungalows showing Japanese influence at the western end of Long Island were exotics; and the attempt at gardening consistent with the architecture of the one and the other's disregard of the matter are of little consequence to the movement.

Figs. 44, 49, 54, 56

Fig. 50, Frontis.

Figs. 27, 29, 30, 31

Figs. 58, 63

Louis Sullivan's holiday retreat on Biloxi Bay took full advantage of its semi-tropical location by abounding in lush vegetation. The cottage itself was located on the front half of its narrow lot of more than twelve acres. On a line with the front door was a circular pool, 30 feet in diameter, and between it and the house lay an elliptical flower garden, containing seats, arbors, and open pavilions built of natural cypress, which could be viewed from the veranda. A circular rose garden was to the east and a little back of the house, and other gardens (including one for vegetables) were farther back. There also was a long pool, crossed by a bridge, and a servants' house, stable, wood-house, and chicken house. With some of the elements being on axis with the main house, and curvilinear paths connecting the various parts, the figure presented was strongly reminiscent of a Downing layout, though considerably larger in size.

Fig. 65

Fig. 180

Fig. 28

Landscaping hardly could be more different from the foregoing than in the contemporary Farson house at Oak Park. Maher's is as stark as

Fig. 67

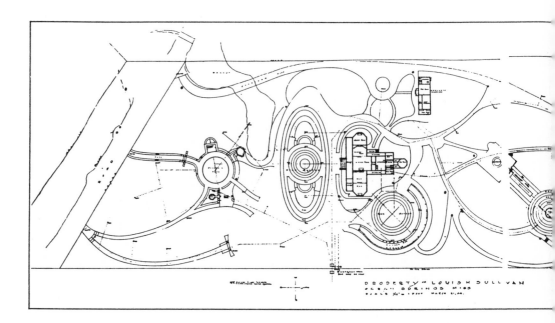

Fig. 71

Sullivan's is luxuriant, in sympathy with the contrast in the style of the building and its radiating walkways. At the Illinois house, mature trees are tolerated at a distance, the scant planting in proximity consisting of palms in a small median bed of the promenade to the main entrance, and palms accompanied by vines in a pair of urns to either side, plus another pair on the balcony of the house. The use of tropical plants indicates that even these were only seasonal ornaments.

Verdure around the fully developed prairie house was equally calculated as in the Farson scheme, though more abundant. In the residence Wright conceived for the *Ladies' Home Journal* in 1901 there is a rectangular space interlaying the entrance terrace, driveway, public walk along the street, and private walk to the house, which is filled with yearlong green shrubbery and warm-weather diversely colored flowers, and the building is further spotted with growing things in window boxes and on walls. The plant bed articulates the distance from the street to the house, and, like the last, it remains as much an observable item; it is not a garden in which the owner would dig for pleasure. Although in many respects similar, it is in the unnaturalness of the planting, as well as in the color contrast between stuccoed walls and landscape, wherein the prairie house departs from the true bungalow ideal.

Purcell, Feick and Elmslie's drawings for the Bungalow on the Point show that it was meant to have irregular greenery adjacent to the living-room curve, outside the terminal terraces, and on the upper overhangs

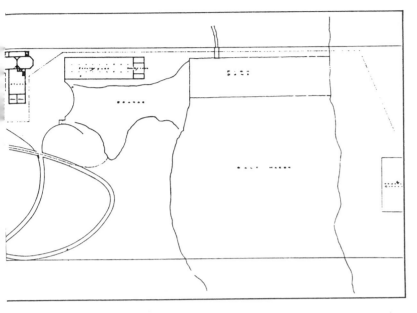

180. Plot Layout of Louis Sullivan's Vacation House, Ocean Springs, Miss. *Architectural Record*, June 1905.

at either end. The present clipped hedge, concentric with the semi-circular pavilion at a 20-foot additional radius, is a later innovation. Like the architecture, the originally planned vegetation was a departure from that of earlier East Coast bungalows.

Fig. 74
Fig. 72

Although developed simultaneously, the California bungalow did not follow the planting scheme of the Chicago School but diverged in proportion to the dissimilarities in building types and setting. The more rustic California bungalow was devised for the country, and if it later was absorbed by suburbia it retained its old garden domain more than it resorted to the style fabricated for lots of this size around the Great Lakes. The squared-off bed shrubbery was all right for the East and Midwest but was not to be endured in California, whereas Downing's Hudson River Valley and Sullivan's Gulf Coast rural offered more acceptable models.

Although rectangular in every aspect of its design, the Bandini bungalow was sufficiently rustic in its parts to justify nonchalant landscaping. Its galleries were paved with stones sunk in poured concrete, like the fireplace hearths, and this material expanded out into the courtyard as an organically shaped walk that was widest around a circular fountain pool in the middle. These elements were edged in cobblestones. A single tree highlighted the court, and incidental plants were allowed to thrive in the leftover spaces, along the flanks of the house, and climb on the pergola.

Figs. 79, 80, 81

Fig. 181

181. Perspective Sketch of the Arturo Bandini Bungalow, Pasadena, Calif. Greene and Greene, Architects. Drawn by the author.

More than half of the Hollister court was paved, and it contained a rectangular pool; the exposed-earth spaces were specifically identified

Fig. 82   as lawns on the plan. The area between the wings of the Tichenor house was two-fifths raised brick terrace, and the yard beyond sloped down to

Fig. 83   a pool spanned by an arched bridge.

The Irwin residence is so much integral with its setting that the first could not be discussed without the second (Chapter Five). Whatever shortcomings the house may have in its interior circulation, it is a masterpiece in the way its shifting angles ease the form into its surrounding

Figs. 86, 88   porches, pergolas, and terraces, and the out-of-doors. The most direct way into the house is via the porte-cochere, which is reached by winding up the driveway, with its ivy-covered wall to the left, affording a full panorama of the long flank of the house, suitably planted, to the right, then proceeding along the covered walk outside the dining room to the side entry, from which one could obtain a view of the other side of the planting next to the building. The pedestrian entrance is along the broad walk from North Grand Avenue; one has the choice of going around to the back of the south terrace and entering by the stairhall or the reception-hall door, or of mounting the steps to the left, crossing the lawn and up another set of steps, to go in the door on the far side of the reception hall. In either of the three routes the visitor is not likely to miss the landscape architecture before entering the building.

The nearby Gamble house and the Pratt house at Nordhoff are as well endowed with surrounding terraces as the Irwin residence. At the Gamble house the front and rear paved areas are only a few feet apart on the north side, with convenient stairs from one to the other. The view from the west terrace over the Arroyo is comparable to that behind the Pratt bungalow of the Ojai.

*Figs. 93,
96, 97*

In the more important Greene and Greene projects the gardening was put in the capable hands of George Chisholm, who had his own nursery.[1] The most extensive landscaping for Pasadena examples here shown was in the six-acre lot of the Blacker house, bounded on the north and east by Hillcrest, and on the west by Wentworth Avenue. The house was set near the northwest corner, with its drive originating at the junction of the two streets. The greater part of the land, therefore, lay to the southeast. A billiard room was in the basement at this corner, which was at ground level. Well removed from the house, in the hollow, a pool was dug and carefully planted, and at one end was elevated an open gazebo. Most of the estate enjoyed the luxury of rolling lawn. A gardener's cottage was provided for the caretaker. The Blacker house currently presides over only a portion (a lot 200-by-220 feet) of the former domain, the balance having been divided into building sites.

Fig. 182

The reader may have noted that the specialized type bungalows, discussed in Chapter Six, are mostly void of horticulture. The adobe house at Santa Fe may be excused, as being in the desert, and perhaps

182. View of Landscaping about the R. R. Blacker House from Pool to Southeast of Residence, Pasadena, Calif. Greene and Greene, Architects. Courtesy of Greene and Greene Library, Pasadena, Calif.

Fig. 119

Fig. 118

*Figs. 126,
127, 128,
135, 137
139, 143*

Fig. 132

newly completed and not yet landscaped when its picture was taken. The perspective of the Ansell retreat shows a backdrop of trees, but little else other than a plateau situation. The log camp in Tennessee, Norwegian house on Chestnut Hill, chalet in Walnut Hills, steamboat house in New Orleans, and the vacation house on the lake in Washington have virtually nothing green in their vicinity. Except for the model house in Kentucky and Greek Revival house made into a bungalow in Alabama, only the two Japanese examples, Shō-fu-den and the Yamanaka competition winner (only one of which actually existed) were given a proper natural setting. Shō-fu-den was erected in an already wooded area. One is tempted to attribute the exceptions to the fact that Far Eastern people are the world's greatest enthusiasts over nature, as illustrated in their paintings (landscape was introduced into European painting only after the return of the Polos from Cathay),[2] their architecture (the curved roof seems to have come into being to harmonize with the lines of hills and trees),[3] their poetry (as shown in its influence upon early-twentieth-century imagists),[4] and in their thinking in general.

The Japanese developed the small court garden, which, as an example of highly evolved proletarian art, equaled the woodblock color print and the Japanese dwelling, to the latter of which it was an adjunct. It became known to the West through Josiah Conder, an Englishman who went to Japan in 1877 as a young architect to teach his profession in the engineering department of the Imperial University, and whose book, *Landscape Gardening in Japan*, was published at London in 1893. The volume was illustrated by facsimiles of old woodcuts and by modern lithographs made by E. Koshima. Also at London in the same year appeared the *Supplement* to the Conder book, being an album of fifty-seven photographs of gardens by K. Ogawa. The two together widened our knowledge of Japanese landscaping in the same way that Edward S. Morse's *Japanese Homes* had done for architecture six or seven years earlier. The gardening book included chapters on its history, planting, composition, and such elements as water, bridges, arbors, lanterns, wells and water basins, and ornamental stones.

Fig. 183

One of the older illustrations reproduced is a garden of a Sakai merchant. A small L-shaped space, traversed by meandering stepping-stone paths, contains rocks and plants artistically arranged, with a great stone lantern as pivotal point, a well to the lower right, a tea house behind a bamboo screen diagonally opposite, and the garden is overlooked by the residence itself in the foreground. The elements were

183. Garden of a Sakai Merchant. Josiah Conder,
Landscape Gardening in Japan, London, 1893.

chosen and arranged to belie the miniature area, which was a factor
adaptable to American bungalow conditions. One sees in this the prototype of the American rock garden.

For those who could not afford their own full- or part-time gardener,
help could be procured from firms and individuals. One, H. H. Bergen
and Company, of New York City, in 1903 issued a catalog of flower bulbs
and such materials as: "Bamboo for bridges, kiosks, stone lanterns,
porcelain pots, dwarfed plants, etc."[5] A few years later the American
and Japanese Nursery Company, Baltimore, offered a free booklet entitled *Gardening Lessons from the Japanese.*[6] Also there were those
who provided services for building gardens. There was the Japanese
Construction Company of Orange, New Jersey.[7] A Japanese gentleman
of Chicago, T. R. Otsuka, announced in 1915 that he had been in business for twenty-four years, executing "all styles" of Nipponese garden
installation "with a specialty to harmonize American ground."[8] The best-
known creator of Japanese landscapes in the New York area at this time
was Takeo Shiota, though his known works exceeded the bungalow
scale.[9]

A house and lot design published in *Bungalow Magazine* in 1910

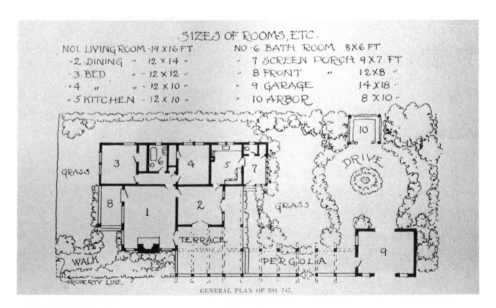

184, 185. Perspective Drawing and Plan of Wilson Bungalow No. 747 for a Suburban Corner Lot. *Bungalow Magazine*, April 1910.

Figs. 184, 185

furnishes us with an ideal small suburban home of the period, "No. 747." Called a "Wilson Bungalow," after the editor, the building is located on a piece of ground measuring 50-by-120 feet; it is set back 14 feet from the street in front and 8 feet on the side. The house contains five rooms, a bath, and two porches. The living and dining rooms open

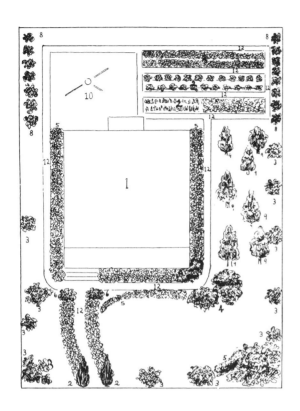

186. "Plan for Planting Spring Garden: No. 1." Gustav Stickley, *More Craftsman Homes*, New York, 1912.

187. Wash Rendering of the House and Landscaping, Spring Garden No. 1. Stickley, *More Craftsman Homes*.

THE AMERICAN BUNGALOW

onto a large screen-walled terrace that connects with a pergola leading to the garage. The latter opens both to the street and the grounds, there being a circular drive that runs to a summerhouse. As in the Sakai merchant's garden, the center motif is a Japanese stone lantern, this one in a grass plot framed by low shrubs. The same greenery accentuates the outer side of the drive, pergola, walk to the back porch, and the lot itself. Inside, the contours are curved, elements are obscured, and planting is irregular, as in the Sakai design. The terrace and pergola correspond to the porch that invariably faces the Japanese garden; and the same sort of circulation unity is achieved. Privacy is assured by a combination of masonry and verdure. Here, in a limited range, is achieved the bungalow dweller's autonomous realm.

Bungalow No. 747 shows how a few artifices may be employed to gain the privacy that larger examples, as on the Blacker and Gamble estates, achieved through remoteness from the public concourse. Fortunately, planting accords with architecture of roof-dominated forms and low-

188. "A Very Simple Rustic Gateway."
Gustav Stickley, *Craftsman Homes*,
New York, 1909.

189. "Gate with Pergola Construction Overhead." Stickley, *Craftsman Homes.*

keyed color schemes and natural materials, and thus the bungalow could use plenty of it gracefully. No matter how small the lot size, the bungalow was removed from the street. It might be half hidden by planting, growing on or against it, sculptured with the bungalow form, as it were, and shrubs and other greenery shielded at least some portion of the yard. This situation brought the bungalow dweller close to his environment, and it encouraged him to perform his own gardening, a factor that would have delighted A. J. Downing. No matter what his occupation, whether a professional man, a white-collar worker, shopkeeper or clerk, or in industry, the horticulture experience would have made the bungalow owner a better-rounded person.

190. "Arbor and Flower Walk in an English Garden." Stickley, *Craftsman Homes*.

191. Arbor Seat. The Long-Bell Lumber Company, Kansas City, Mo., *The Book of Lawn Furniture* (catalog), 1929.

American bungalow-oriented literature included the gardening aspect. In Henry Saylor's book on *Bungalows*, published in 1911, the last chapter, of fifteen pages, was on flora; it included advice not only on where and how to plant, but what time of year as well. Home periodicals presented articles on the subject. *House Beautiful*, which came into existence with the December, 1896, issue, was imitated by a magazine of similar format, *House and Garden*, beginning in June, 1901, that linked setting with building in the title. Gustav Stickley's publications included material on gardening, his *Craftsman Homes* (1909) and *More Craftsman Homes* (1912) containing chapters that had appeared earlier as articles in *The Craftsman* magazine. In a nine-page spread in the second book called "Craftsman Gardens for Craftsman Homes," he proposes four gardened settings for as many bungalows, each 40-feet square on 75-by-100-foot lots. They are primed as the four blooming "seasons," spring, early summer, late summer, and autumn. Each included ornamental and useful plants, the latter in the form of a rectangular vegetable garden. The kitchen squares adjoin the house in all four cases, and in the second and third examples they are in front. The early-summer version screens the vegetable garden from the street by a vine-covered trellis, and in the late-summer version only by planting rows of tall corn in the foreground. Each of these proposals is illustrated by a wash perspective drawing and a plan. The house is set square on the site in the Spring Garden. Small cedars are at the entrance and hardy flowers border the walk that curves up to the front porch and encircles the house. Shrubs frame the yard, leaving an intervening front *Fig. 186* lawn, and dwarf fruit trees fill the side yard. The kitchen garden and a drying ground are behind. The accompanying view does all a rendering could do to make the layout appealing, but in accomplishing this it exaggerates distances, such as the size of the front and side yards. *Fig. 187* Much the same elements appear in all four of the gardens. Cedars are stationed at the beginning of the paths; rose bushes flank two and a Japanese barberry hedge the other one; there is a small grove of fruit trees, and shrubs fill corners. The Fall Garden has a grape arbor along one side of the house. The arrangements are Downingesque, reduced to a minimum. They are executed in much less space and in less taste. *Fig. 28*

Of all the chapters having to do with outdoor settings in *Craftsman Homes*, that on garden gates comes closest to the craftsmanship theme. There are three types. The simplest is a contrived rusticity, using natural materials, as in the stick fence in front of the remodeled house at

Fig. 45
Fig. 188

Fig. 189

Fig. 190

Fig. 191

Falmouth. Stickley's example consists of upright sapling posts joined by a "peaked hood," with a picket gate. A second type relates better to the average bungalow. Called a "pergola gate," it is composed of squared timbers of various sizes and left unpainted, having an arbor at the top to support vines. The text notes that its "straight unornamented lines suggest an inspiration from Japan," and the photograph was taken before planting was developed "to give a clear idea of the construction." The third type is represented by a roofed trellis with arches, described as a "flower walk in an English garden, affording not only a pleasant summer retreat but also a most attractive vista through the large grounds." This structure, reminiscent of extensive layout in eighteenth-century formal gardens of the Old World, was the least appropriate to the scale and temperament of the bungalow, or to the informal garden.

Like the box bungalow itself, the last species of landscape ornament was developed into a mass-production commodity that disrupted the proper bungalow environment. Manufacturers issued not only gateways and pergolas, fences, and trellises, but seats, swings, dog houses, bird houses, aviaries and other cages, and playful wind devices—geese with thrashing wings, miniature windmills, and sunflowers that revolve crazily. Latticework was lavished on these garden encroachments, and practically all of it was painted stark white (except for the sunflowers). Such conceits were a far cry from the use of proper rock and cobblestone walls, stick and stained wood fences, gates and benches, which tied in with natural surroundings. Catalog-ordered outdoor furniture, like houses similarly provided, were major factors in bringing about the expiration of the bungalow and its setting.

NOTES

1. Clay Lancaster, "My Interviews with Greene and Greene," *Journal of the American Institute of Architects*, July 1957, pp. 202–206.

2. I. V. Pouzyna, *La Chine, l'Italie et les Débuts de la Renaissance (XIIIe–XIVe Siècles)*, Paris, 1935.

3. Clay Lancaster, "The Origin and Formation of Chinese Architecture," *Journal of the Society of Architectural Historians*, March–May 1950, p. 10.

4. Earl Miner, *The Japanese Tradition in British and American Literature*, Princeton, 1958, pp. 157–182.

5. *Country Life in America*, October 1903, p. 472.

6. *Ibid.*, March 1908, p. 545.

7. *Ibid.*, October 1903, p. 472.

8. *Ibid.*, February 1915, p. 7.

9. Clay Lancaster, *The Japanese Influence in America*, New York, 1963, pp. 198–200, 205.

X

A SUMMING UP AND AN EVALUATION OF THE AMERICAN BUNGALOW

THE BUNGALOW in the United States was a type of house, a period of architecture, and a movement. In terms of the first category it can be recognized by its form, which is low, overshadowed by the roof, restrained in the matter of style, subdued in color, and blended with its setting. Considered as a period, the title bungalow can be given to all detached residential buildings produced during the first quarter of the twentieth century, and to others related to them that belong in the two decades before and almost a decade after that twenty-five-year interval. As a movement the building of bungalows was governed by principles such as simplicity, vitality, and straightforwardness, and these applied to every aspect of the phenomenon: its exterior and its affinity to its environment, the relation between outside and inside, its interior and how it best could serve the purpose of sheltering and providing a pleasant atmosphere for the modern family.

In this last sense the American bungalow was the counterpart of Art Nouveau, which enjoyed exactly the same time span in Europe. They were equally innovative. Both Art Nouveau in the Old World and the bungalow in the New World touched on a broad field extending from man's habitation to everything in it on which the artistic faculty could be brought to bear. The difference was in where the emphasis was placed: the bungalow concentrated on dwellings and only secondarily dealt with their furnishings, whereas the province of Art Nouveau primarily had to do with decorative arts, including interiors in general, and only occasionally enveloped the whole building. As with the bungalow, when edifices were involved, Art Nouveau was not likely to resort to a strictly architectural treatment. But also, Art Nouveau had as much—or more—to do with public as with domestic buildings.[1]

Art Nouveau attempted to achieve significance through seeking out fresh sources of inspiration, solving problems candidly, and giving originality free rein. As one of its foremost leaders said, for a people "to counterfeit the genius of their ancestors . . . [was] to sterilize the genius of their own generation"; rather they should seek "beneath the accumulated ashes of old systems the spark of that former life which had developed the arts of the people." The author of these lines, Siegfried Bing, was invited by the government to come to the United States and make a study of its industrial arts; and the statement was in an early issue of *The Craftsman*, edited and published by Gustav Stickley, whose bungalow connections have been noted.[2] Art Nouveau took on contradistinctive characteristics according to place and its individual creators. As we have seen, the American bungalow was equally diverse. Perhaps the nearest thing to a signature motif in Art Nouveau was the whiplash line; but by no means did it appear on all or even on the largest percentage of its products. It was the same with the bungalow features, those mentioned in the second sentence in this chapter. It is significant that both Art Nouveau and the bungalow sought inspiration in the art and architecture of the Far East.[3] The source was mainly Japan. This was partly due to the recent discovery of that remarkable culture, fulfilling a search for newness, but mainly it was because a rich and seemingly inexhaustible field of high aesthetic quality had been tapped. Contemporary Impressionist painting benefited from the same fount. As Art Nouveau represented the decorative-arts handmaiden of Impressionism in European fine arts, both of which were felt only nominally in America, the foremost expression of the artistic ferment in the United States was the bungalow in its sundry aspects.

Due to the novel attitude of being emancipated from tradition current throughout the Western World at the close of the nineteenth century, bungalow builders were able to achieve an end that had been anticipated by A. J. Downing before mid century. Some of Downing's plans were very modern for their day, and his bracketed cottage was allied with (but not quite married to) its setting, foreshadowing the bungalow. However, his architecture, and certainly his furniture, retained a good deal of handed-down ornamentation for no greater reason than romantic adherence—a lurking psychological dependence that was not quite realistic. Romanticism had to run its course before the bungalow could emerge.

The first American bungalows appeared on the Atlantic Seaboard, nearest England, whence the concept came. But, except for that one unique early specimen by Schweinfurth at Newton Centre, this region merely toyed with application of the name "bungalow" without developing a real fabric. The central states on the Great Lakes fashioned a tangible image but was reluctant to give it anything but a geographic designation. At least the firm of Purcell, Feick and Elmslie was not so biased as to withhold the term from their Prairie–New England hybrid, the Bungalow on the Point. It was California that came forward with the definition and definitive form taken by the American bungalow. The newly arrived Greene brothers raised it to the beaux-arts level, giving to it a higher status in the United States than it achieved elsewhere in the world. Like architects of the Chicago School they conceived buildings on the organic principle, bestowing first consideration upon the functioning form. Both Central and Western buildings contained parts integral with each other, and the whole to the site, but the visible structure of the bungalow acquired warmth and a more personable effect than had the prairie house. The California bungalow became organic in the sense of being something greater, more fluid and lifelike, than geometry, and it was this organic quality, thoroughly integrated inside and outside, that placed the bungalow among the top achievements in American architecture.

If the informal living room did not originate with the bungalow, at least it came into full potency in it. Here the living room was not just another interior, substituting for a parlor or dining room, as heretofore, but it was the very heart and core of the house, regulating its pulse and the outflowing of life that animated it. The rest of the rooms—dining room, kitchen, bedrooms, and bath—were given over to care for the family's creature needs; but the living room was where the residents and their friends consorted together, where they indulged in conversation, participated in literature, music, and the other arts, where they read in solitude or relaxed, where, in short, they delved into the more refined, the more penetrating aspects of human existence.

The living room usually adjoined and connected with a porch or terrace, onto which its functions were transferred outdoors when weather permitted. The easily accessible garden was an intimate floriculture spot, inviting one to plant and cultivate, to pluck blossoms for buttonhole or dining-table decoration; the garden was an adjunct to the bungalow, a sharer in its life. The bungalow garden was quite different from traditional architectural landscaping, being not so formalized, nearer to unprocessed nature, and by its character it tied in no less successfully with the equally different type of building to which it related. It presented the bungalow dweller a microcosm of this planet Earth, over which the philosopher and poet in him might wonder and versify, the explorer and scientist seek, and the despot rule.

The autocracy of the bungalow domain—however small—through

the new type of privacy it afforded, made every owner his castle's baron. Yet the bungalow ideal of environmental submersion made for a neighborhood unity, which is infinitely more pleasing than the staccato effect of suburban developments today. Bungalow designers maintained the essence of the natural topography in the wake of expanding subdivisions. Those not properly indoctrinated were restrained by the lack of bulldozers, backhoes, and other monstrous nature-defacing instruments that we have. Bungalow houses were built specifically for people, and not for their automobiles. There were no cars during the early bungalow period, and after they came in they were sheltered in small garages at the back of the lot, where the stable and carriage house had stood formerly. The effect was unlike that of the present house, wherein the carport or garage, with its big, ugly doors, is out in front.

During those halcyon days when phonographs were scarce, and before radios and televisions were rampant, not to overlook droning air-conditioners, living in proximity to other people was still an agreeable experience. There were no noise problems such as we have. Our solution is to box ourselves in a soundproof house shell. Soundproofing, of course, benefits only those inside, as everybody within earshot is tormented by the whirring mechanisms. One shudders at how impossible it would be to use a bungalow sleeping porch next door to a temperature-controlled building. Besides, the house with the artificial atmosphere is diametrically opposed to the bungalow's intimacy with nature. Withdrawing ourselves from seasonal changes is being deprived of one of the chief rewards that our stay in this world affords.

The established American community, which had come into existence from the seventeenth up into the nineteenth century, reached its limits while yet maintaining its integrity during the bungalow period. By 1900 its chief transportation facility consisted of a system of electric trolleys, which was expanded to convey bungalow lodgers downtown and home again. Thus, the city pattern, of civic and commercial nucleus, and residential perimeter, was preserved. It was later, when the suburbs magnified overwhelmingly, and outpost shopping centers sprang up within them to claim their business, that the urban character became confused. Main Street lost its magnetism. People gravitated to the new conveniences. The shopping mall is a squat, monotonous line of cheaply constructed buildings running alongside acres of asphalt paving for parking. It is devoid of greenery, but there are plenty of automobiles with their poisonous odors. The United States ranks first in the world as a nation of drivers, of inhabitants lacking physical contact with their environment. Roadways start at the house (garage) door; they radiate out and are enmeshed across the country leading to work, markets, social and educational institutions, recreation and amusement facilities, including that paved parking place for pleasure, the drive-in cinema. All of this outlay is sprawling and wasteful of space and resources, harsh and vacuous without people to animate it, and devoid of intrinsic human amenities.

The bungalow stood for a more civilized existence. Its heyday corresponded with the apex of democratic domestic architecture in the United States. It is unfortunate that the commercialized disintegration of the bungalow dragged its good name down to such degraded depths, but at least we can be thankful that the term was not perpetuated and applied to the sterile and shoddy structure that succeeded the box bungalow phase. Further, it is gratifying to perceive in the few appealing homes built in modern times that their qualities derive from the sound principles evolved for the bungalow classic.

NOTES

1. Art Nouveau was popularized at European international fairs, beginning with the lounge created by Henry Van de Velde at the Dresden Exposition of 1897, and including the Pavillon Bleu and Art Nouveau Bing at the Paris Exposition of 1900, the Central Rotunda at the Turin Exposition of 1902, and the Central Hall (again by Van de Velde) at the Dresden Exposition of 1906. These led to the shaping of permanent establishments (such as S. Bing's Art Nouveau emporium) in the same style in the cities.

2. S. Bing, "L'Art Nouveau," translated from the French by Irene Sargent, The Craftsman, October 1903, p. 3.

3. Clay Lancaster, "Oriental Contributions to Art Nouveau," The Art Bulletin, December 1952, pp. [297]–311.

APPENDIX

MY FATHER'S
BUNGALOW (1914),
LEXINGTON, KENTUCKY

192. John William Lancaster II Bungalow, Lexington, Ky.
Perspective drawing by the author.

LIKE THOMAS JEFFERSON, my father, John W. Lancaster II, was never happier than when building, and it seemed to make little difference to him whether what he was working on was a house that he or somebody else was to live in. He had hardly finished his second home, since being married, in the newly laid-out Bell Court, when he began the one in which he was to reside for the rest of his life. It was on a larger, two-lot site (100-by-150 feet) around the corner, facing south. Perhaps because my mother (although trained as a classical concert pianist) was a modernist in all things visual (and practical), the new home was to be in the most advanced bungalow style. John V. Moore was the architect. Moore was distinguishing himself as a designer of bungalows not only at Lexington but at Mt. Sterling, Danville, and Paris, Kentucky, at Ashville, North Carolina, and by one commission for an "American Bungalow" as far away as Gloucestershire, England.

The preliminary drawings John V. Moore made were on a sheet (13⅜-by-33⅛ inches) of heavy oiled paper, which now has become brown with age, so that the pencil delineations are barely discernible. They consist of two floor plans, and front and east elevations, the latter embellished by ornamental planting, all scaled one-eighth inch to the foot. Floor-plan walls were filled in with crayon, orange to denote masonry (outside walls and chimneys of brick) and yellow for frame (inside partitions, bay window, dormers, and the staircase). Except for the addition of a fireplace in the upstairs east chamber, the design was approved and enlarged for the final blueprints. It is interesting that the front suite in the preliminary drawing was composed of dining room, reception hall, and parlor, and that the room behind the last was labeled "living room." The formality of the south rooms, with colonnades separating the units, justified calling the one with the fireplace a parlor. Although it was inscribed "living room" on the final plans it was used as a parlor, which means very seldom, and only on "dress" occasions. Moore was prophetic in calling the second room the living room; we called it the "sitting room," and it was here we spent most of our time together. It served as an infirmary on the rare occasions when one of us was sufficiently ill to require nursing, and, rarer still, as a guest chamber when we had overnight visitors. As a child I used to wrap up in my heaviest sweater, sneak off to the arctic clime of the living room—parlor in all but name—curl up in the overstuffed wingchair, and read my Christmas books. Here I was sure of not being disturbed.

The final drawings for the house were rendered into six sheets (15-by-28 inches) of blueprints, consisting of (1) basement, (2) first-floor and (3) second-floor plans, (4) facade and rear, (5) east and (6) west elevations, with a cross-section of the reception hall, showing the fireplace on the east wall of the living room on sheet no. 2, and an elevation of the first flight of the staircase on sheet no. 3. These were scaled one-quarter inch to the foot. There also were interior-beam profiles for the front rooms, exterior-cornice and structural details. The sheets are dated 20 April 1914.

Fig. 192 The roof was covered with red terra-cotta, German tile, and it over-hung two feet on all sides. A bedroom projected as a large gabled dormer in front, its roofline dipping, like that of the principal roof, and abutments to either side of the front-porch steps curved similarly. The upper walls were of stucco applied to brick, except for the dormers (front and back),which were of stucco on wire lath nailed to the wood framework. Basement walls were laid of quarried limestone or rubble, and the stonework was given a struck joint above grade. A row of yellow bricks, set upright (lettered "Brick Soldier Course" on the elevation drawings), slightly projecting, capped the brickwork. The stucco was painted buff, and trim was mostly maroon. Lower window sills, exterior steps, and porch parapet and curved abutment copings were of cut limestone. The Tuscan porch colonnettes were of wood, sand-painted gray to resemble stone.

Fig. 193 The plans here shown are as I first remember the house. The front suite was impressive, with ninety-inch-tall columns flanking the hall, ten-foot-high ceilings having heavy interlacing beams overhead, pan-eled wainscot with plate rail and a window-seat recess in the dining room, and an arched brick fireplace and colonnetted mantel, with a paneled chimneybreast above, in the living room. The projecting fire-place was flanked by small square windows in the east wall, beneath which was a pair of mahogany bookcases with glass doors that lifted and slid back over the books. The front windows were five-feet wide. The entrance doorway had leaded beveled glass in the elliptical fan and sidelights; and, facing south (actually southwest), the low afternoon

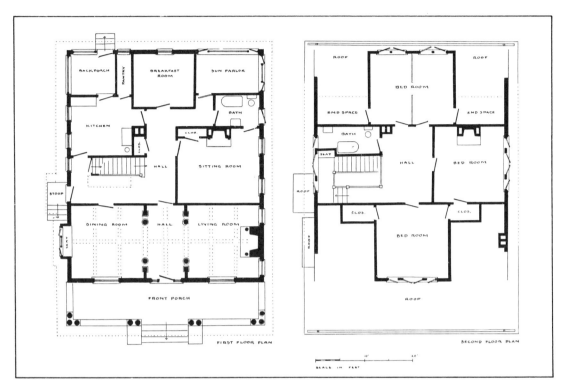

193. First- and Second-floor Plans of the Lancaster Bungalow. Drawn by the author.

sun sent rainbows stealing slowly across the far walls. Although Moore's final plans (like the earlier sketch) show a door connecting the living room and sitting room behind, it was eliminated before construction began. The other first-floor change was in the small room centered at the rear. In Moore's drawing it was a "child's room," with a narrow strip cut off from the west side for a closet to this room and another to the kitchen. The closets were not realized, and the room always was the family's "breakfast room," actually where we ate all of our meals. A hatch to a cellar entrance was proposed under the room's window; it was deleted at the time of building, but a basement door, preceded by a glass-covered areaway, and concrete steps to one side, later resulted from a kennel established below stairs, for one of my father's numerous hobbies—this one was raising Boston terriers.

Moore's second-story plan showed a permanent partition dividing the wide Dutch dormer at the back into two "sleeping porches." As built, the division was a thin wall of wood panels, which was removed when I was young, and at the same time the easternmost of the two doors to the hall was closed, the doorway itself moved a few feet to connect with the adjoining bedroom. My brother and I were given the back room, and, a few years later, the two "end spaces" were plastered and finished so that each of us could have his private hideaway. Later they became the means of preserving a remarkably complete set of post-World-War-I-period children's playthings, including stuffed animals, lead soldiers, cast-iron and wind-up toys, construction sets, Humpty Dumpties, and electric trains.

The only other change made, while I was still small, was the installation of double glazed doors between the breakfast room and sun parlor. The architect has called the latter a "solarium" on his plan, and a "French door" opened to the hall, which, due to its several bendings, was dark at this end, even with glass in the door. All of the solarium fenestration was to have been stationary, whereas the sun parlor that materialized had casements at either end of both windows. These, the bathroom window downstairs, and all upstairs casements had flyscreens inside, all capable of being opened. The first-story windows with double-hung sashes had flyscreen frames that hooked on the outside, except for the two in the sitting room, which had louvered shutters that were closed every night, and these had adjustable screens to insert under a lifted sash. The back porch had lattices in the openings, and after the old icebox was supplanted by an electric refrigerator, glazed units were set inside the lattices, including one in the outside door. These were hinged and could be entirely removed in the summertime.

The only inside trim that was painted was in the downstairs bathroom. It was white, like the ceramic mosaic hexagons in the floor, the glazed-tile of the four-foot wainscot, and the walls and ceiling. The remaining woodwork in the house was given a natural finish. That in the front suite was a dark red cherry, or (as in the case of the columns) of another wood stained to match. The flooring here was oak, given a birch finish. Other visible wood in the house, including the floors, was of yellow pine, stained and varnished. Interior doors downstairs contained two upright panels, those upstairs had five horizontal panels, both being standard mill-produced designs. Casings consisted of simple uprights, slightly rounded at the corners, supporting a plain fascia capped by a cornice. The staircase was in the craftsman–mission style, with square newel posts, closed stringer, square banisters, and a shaped handrail. Walls and ceiling in the front rooms were painted John Lancaster buff. The kitchen, back porch, sun parlor, and upstairs bath were the same color. Elsewhere the rooms were papered in a series of patterns too varied to characterize, but the background was usually buff.

The house was heated by a coal-burning, hot-air furnace in the cellar, with ducts to registers in the floor of every room in the main story excepting the pantry. The opening beneath the stairwell was supposed to heat the second story, but in cold weather it had to be supplemented by gas burners in the bedrooms and upstairs bath. A gas stove sat in the front of the metal plate that closed the sitting-room fireplace, to warm this room on chilly mornings while the furnace was being stoked. The other two fireplaces had gas logs.

The lawn was sown in bluegrass. An ancient hackberry tree was left standing near the southwest corner of the house in the front yard. Split by a windstorm during the late 1930s, it had to be taken down. An arbor of stained redwood, for grape vines of several varieties, was set up to either side of the driveway in the backyard, extending from the wooden arch over the gate in the division fence to the garage. This structure grew from a single-car stall to a three-car garage with stairway and second story for storage and my father's pigeons. Like the house, it was of yellow brick and stucco. A wire fence encircled the back yard. I remember early hen houses, a vegetable garden, and fruit trees. They were replaced by a formal rose garden having a concentric-circular plan northeast of the house. The garden received little attention after the Boston-terrier colony passed the dozen count. The typical bungalow planting was that set out around the front porch and sides, consisting of a double row of evergreens and flowering shrubs; hemlocks were planted next to the abutments flanking the steps and at the porch corners, with low junipers beyond, mahonia and abelia between them, and spirea, syringa, and hydrangea on the flanks. Their beds were given a wavy contour at the greensward line. Maple trees were spaced across the lot, and a hedge was kept trimmed next to the concrete sidewalk and along the sides.

Bell Court was a subdivision of about forty acres, of which a four-acre block in the center was reserved for Woodside, a Greek Revival mansion that had been constructed for Henry Bell during the 1840s. Inasmuch as the whole neighborhood was built at about the same time, mostly by young married couples, there were many children in my age bracket, and the pasture behind the mansion was an ideal place for flying kites and organized games. Many old trees (like our hackberry) had been preserved, and many young trees and shrubs had been added, so that the general aspect was lush and green. The main entrance to Bell Court was a short, wide avenue leading off Main Street on axis with Woodside. Other entrances were at the southwest and northeast corners, but little through traffic traversed the section.

The electric streetcar, which came down Main Street, picked up passengers at Bell Court, and it was a five-minute ride to downtown Lexington. Before World War II the trolleys were replaced by motor buses, and one wound diagonally through Bell Court. The elementary school I attended was less than six blocks away, and the only dangerous crossing (to a little boy), due to traffic, was outside the limits of Bell Court. Going to junior high school entailed a long trek across town. Afterwards, Henry Clay (Senior) High School was a short run of four blocks, due to a recently made cut through the southeast corner of Bell Court. The University of Kentucky was a little over a mile away, but most of the route was along tree-lined residential streets and it was a pleasant walk. I often detoured a few blocks farther, coming home, to go through natural-landscaped Woodland Park, especially in the fall, when the maple leaves were amber and gold, and the sun shone luxuriously through the tree branches.

Our house was only a fifteen-minute walk from the courthouse. When I came from downtown, along Main Street, with its noise and smell of traffic, a great peace settled over me as I turned into the quiet of Bell Court. Many people walked, in those days, and people sat on their front porches in the late afternoons and evenings, talking and visiting, while the children played together in the yard. Sometimes we could persuade my mother to perform on the piano in the living room, and some of us would sing. It was a friendly, sociable atmosphere. People lived just close enough together and just far enough apart, and the neighborhood was agreeably cloaked in verdancy.

INDEX

Italicized page numbers refer to illustrations and floor plans.